A bunch of guys slammed into the diner suddenly and started making a big scene. Without turning around, I recognized the voices.

"Russell Randolph," I said to Chels. "Paul Wong. Corey Talbott." They hang around together at school. You hardly ever see them apart. "They're all wearing the same kind of jeans and big T-shirts. Right?"

Chels giggled. "Right-o. They're cute, though."

I sighed and turned to look.

What a mess. Seventh-grade boys on the loose are not a pretty sight. They had taken over a booth, where they were bouncing around and laughing and spilling water.

The girls in the booth behind them were pretending not to notice, but they were talking awfully loud and shrieking once in a while, as if someone had pinched them. It made me sick.

When I was a kid, I decided something important. Before my hormones or whatever got out of control, I determined that I would never be one of those girls who giggles around boys. It's disgusting.

## The Victoria Mahoney Series
by Shelly Nielsen

# MORE VICTORIA

**Shelly Nielsen**

**Chariot Books**
DAVID C. COOK PUBLISHING CO.

A White Horse Book
Published by Chariot Books,
an imprint of David C. Cook Publishing Co.
David C. Cook Publishing Co., Elgin, Illinois
David C. Cook Publishing Co., Weston, Ontario

MORE VICTORIA

Cover illustration by Gail Roth
Design by Barbara Sheperd Tillman

Printed in the United States of America
90 89 88 87      5 4 3 2

Library of Congress Cataloging-in-Publication Data
Nielsen, Shelly, 1958-
    More Victoria.
    (A White horse book)
    Summary: Vic's first semester at junior high brings her
worries: a rowdy but popular guy has a crush on her, she
gets sent to the principal's office for misbehaving, and her
parents begin arguing.
    I. Title.
PZ7.N5682Mo 1986      [Fic]      86-2280
ISBN 0-89191-453-6

for Rodney and Darlene,
a couple of experts in the art of parenting
and
for Lois, who's been like a mother

# 1

I saw the note coming.

Connie passed it to Juan, who sneaked it to Brenda, who passed it to Lara. Lara waited till Mrs. Hartford turned her back.

"It's for you," she hissed, tossing it at me. She sounded jealous.

"Vickie Mahoney," it said, right on the front. I unfolded the note and took a look, ignoring the snickering.

*Corey likes you! No joke.*

The laughing stopped. Mrs. Hartford's eyes were scanning the room like radar. She was also twisting

7

her earring, an almost sure sign of trouble. She can *smell* trouble in second period math, even before anyone has thought of something terrible to do. I scrunched in my seat, trying to look invisible.

"What's all the chatter about?" she demanded.

Mrs. Hartford can't stand noise, not even a peep. I have a theory that her husband plays the tuba, and she comes to school every day to get some peace and quiet.

"Students, *please*. Your attention is essential if you have any hopes of ever understanding decimals. Kindly lend me your eyes and ears."

Warning #1.

I tried to pay attention. But after a note like that, math is the probably the last thing your brain wants to think about.

It's not that Corey's terrifically good looking. He's okay. He has nice teeth, for one thing. And very nice eyelashes. But ever since I've been at Keats Junior High, he's been big news. Everyone treats him like a star or something. By the end of the first day, practically by the time I got my locker assignment, I knew all about him.

"What'd the note say?" Lara asked under her breath, sneaking a look at the it.

I folded it up and slid it between the pages of my book. "Not much," I whispered back, which was the truth.

Mrs. Hartford's nose wiggled. "Class!"

Warning #2.

8

I sat up straight. I acted like decimals are the most interesting subject in the world.

Between third and fourth period my friend Chelsie Bixler declared the day a Special Occasion.

"—because I have something amazing I have to tell you," she screamed at me as I passed her in the hall. "Meet me."

"Meet me" meant going to Dahlia's Diner after school, where we celebrate all special occasions (and disasters, too). Dahlia's just happens to be between Chelsie's house and mine. It's very convenient. Cheap, too.

Telling Chelsie about my note was practically all I thought about until the final bell rang, releasing me from Keats Junior Prison. I walked fast to my locker. Chels would know what to do.

"Hurry," she said, shuffling stuff around in her locker, right next to mine. "You won't believe what happened."

We barely talked all the way to Dahlia's except for me saying I had to stop home and ask my neighbors to watch my little brother until I got back. My mom works until five o'clock, and Dad works most evenings, so I'm in charge of Matthew a lot. Chels said she'd go ahead and get our usual table. I hurried; it didn't take me long to get to Dahlia's.

"Hey, Old Vic! Over here!" Chels yelled at me from our usual booth. She even waved her arm around, just in case anyone in the entire restaurant hadn't caught who was screaming across the tables. Blushing purple, or at least a healthy shade of lavender, I slammed into the booth.

"Chels, you don't always have to make a big scene."

Chelsie just grinned. She's always been dramatic, on account of wanting to be an actress, but she's even worse since she joined the Keats Drama Club in September. I think they encourage this sort of thing in the drama club.

"I'm dying to tell you," she said. "Grant Hirshfield said hi to me after choir."

"Are you sure he was talking to *you*?" I didn't mean this the way it sounded. It's just that I know from experience that Grant is very careful about whom he says hi to. He looks like he belongs on a golf course. He probably even irons his jeans, for Pete's sake.

"He said 'Hi, Chelsie.' Is that good enough?"

I didn't blame her for being mad. "Sorry," I said. "That's great." Sometimes it's hard to be constantly excited about the guys who say hi to Chelsie. Chels is what is known as cute. But she is not stuck up or anything. She's my best friend.

The waitress, a high schooler, came to take our order. I skimmed the menu. It was mimeographed off, to remind you of a fifties diner, and there were all kinds of typos in it. You could get stuff like "corned beff hash" or an Ovaltine malt. I ordered my usual.

"A Coke? All you want is a Coke?" The waitress rolled her eyes.

"Baby-sitting funds are kind of on the low side," I explained.

"Give me a turtle sundae," said Chels.

The waitress took off for the kitchen.

"Have I got something to show you," I said, digging in my purse. I handed my note over to her. Chelsie read it three times. I watched her eyes move. Was I nervous. By the time she finished, I had ripped my napkin into bite-size morsels.

"Vic, this is great! This is your ticket into all the great cliques. Pretty soon you'll be at every party, talking to all the right people—"

"Cut it out," I interrupted. It was depressing. She was sounding like Peggy Hiltshire.

Peggy is a sort-of friend of ours. She can be awfully boy crazy sometimes, but other times she's kind of funny to have around.

"It's probably just a joke, anyway," I said. "Guys like Corey Talbott don't hang around with people like me."

"Here's my advice, Victoria. Never assume that you're not this guy's idea of the perfect girl friend. Boys are strange; you can't trust them. They tell you one thing and they're thinking just the opposite. For instance, remember that guy who used to chase you around at recess in the third grade?"

"Wally Humpfinkel? He was weird."

"You thought he hated you."

"He *told* me he hated me. Besides, why else would some kid chase me around the playground every lunch hour?"

"You still don't get it, Vic. He chased you because he liked you. He'd probably still be chasing you if you hadn't blabbed to your mom."

"She said if he didn't quit it she'd come to school and chase *him*." I giggled, imagining my mother running after Wally Humpfinckel.

"And you *told* him. Vic, you were hopeless then, and you're hopeless now."

Our order came.

"Anything else I can get you?" The waitress gave me another look and sauntered away.

I sat back and took a long, cold drink. Junior high was sure interesting. Up until a couple of months ago, Chels and I hardly got *near* any boys. Now they were part of everyday conversation. It was kind of exciting to get mysterious notes—even if they were phony.

"Listen," Chels said, "we've got to get organized." She ripped a clean sheet of paper out of her notebook and uncapped her Flair. "Have you followed your leads?"

"What are leads?"

Chelsie rolled her eyes, doing a pretty good imitation of the waitress. "You call yourself a writer? Any good reporter would do a little investigating, like asking around if anyone's heard rumors about this Corey character falling madly in love with you. Maybe he first knew it was love the day you wore your turquoise skirt. Or maybe when he first saw you scrape your tray in the lunchroom." She started giggling, and pretty soon she was gasping for breath.

I didn't think it was all that funny.

"Sorry, Vic." She cleared her throat and looked serious. "What you should do is try to track down the letter writer." She shook the folded note in my face. "For instance, have you analyzed the handwriting? No, you haven't. I would have analyzed the handwriting."

I squinted at the paper. It was a round, unfamiliar style, with little o's dotting the i's.

Chels paused to scoop a dripping spoonful of hot fudge, ice cream, and peanuts into her mouth and make an appreciative face. Then she said, "I'll help you. Since you're a writer, you follow up the handwriting lead." She wrote *handwriting = Vic* on the paper. "I'll ask around school about Corey. I'll talk to everyone who might have a clue. Maybe I'll even ask *him*."

"DON'T YOU DARE!"

Chels choked on chocolate. "Don't worry," she said, laughing. "I'll be very discreet."

While I finished her sundae, Chels pulled a magazine out of her backpack. We ignored the looks the waitress was flashing our way.

"The latest issue of *Cat Capers*," she announced, handing it over.

13

Cats are our newest interest. I have a cat, a big orange one called Bullrush. Bullrush likes chopped olives and cream cheese on Ritz crackers. He is a culinary cat, because my father is a chef and experiments on him a lot. The only other thing Bullrush likes is sleep, which he does on unmade beds—mostly mine.

Chelsie's parents, especially her mom, won't let her have a cat. Mrs. Bixler likes having a picked-up house. She would die if she ever came to our house; the cat hair practically billows into the corners. But Chels is working on them, slowly but surely. According to her, it's just a matter of time.

Meanwhile, we're reading all about cats. We've found out a lot of interesting and a lot of gross stuff. Like what they eat, how they have kittens, all the different breeds. You'd never believe all the breeds of cats there are. There's a lot to cover, so when we're not talking about boys, we're talking about cats. We used to be into stamps.

"Look on page twenty-four," Chels said. "There's a cat show coming to the Civic Center in a couple weeks. We should go."

"—And enter Bullrush!" I blurted.

She screamed. It's a habit she's gotten into—screaming. Normally I would have been embarrassed, but I felt a little like screaming, too. It was a terrific idea.

"That's perfect!" She stopped suddenly. "Except—what *is* Bullrush, exactly? He's not a full-fledged anything. He's just a mix."

"Here's a category for him: Household Pets. See, it's a special contest for not-purebred cats. He'll win, easy."

"He's kind of fat," Chels said, suddenly doubtful.

"I'll put him on a diet. I'll brush him every day and feed him cod liver oil until his coat shines. He'll be the handsomest cat in Minnesota."

"Wait till I tell Peggy. She'll die. She thinks we're weird as it is."

Come to think of it, Peggy would be a good person to ask about the Corey note. Peg prides herself on knowing all the inside scoops around school.

Chels started gathering up books. "I gotta go. Mom wants me home at a reasonable hour—her words. And I promised I'd pick up squash on the way home. I hate squash, but I'm going to show my parents how dependable I am if it kills me. They don't know it yet, but all this is leading up to me getting that kitten. By December, if I'm lucky. Maybe as a Christmas present. I've been so responsible lately it would make you sick. Come on; walk me to the store."

# 2

Super Savings Supermarket was decorated for Halloween. The checkout clerks all wore buttons that said, "Boo!" Chels and I checked out their special pumpkin display. I almost bought a dimpled pumpkin that reminded me of Mrs. Hartford, but it was too big to lug all the way home. Besides, our stop at Dahlia's had taken most of my funds. I am not what you'd call loaded. So I just wandered around while Chelsie shopped.

I hardly recognized Peter when I backed into him on the candy aisle. Peter is a guy I met in a summer writing course. It had been a long time since I'd seen him. Practically since August.

"You look different," I said, squinting at him. I

was probably just about to say something else just as stupid when he said,

"Really?"

He did look different. Sad. Or something.

"Well, sort of," I said, sorry I had brought up the subject. Tacky, Victoria. Like telling someone who's just gotten over the flu that he looks terrible. "I haven't seen you around much," I said, to cover up.

"I've been pretty busy. Going home after school, mostly."

"Do you ever write things anymore?"

"No." He shrugged. "Gave it up for soccer."

"Which team?"

"The Black & Blue Bruisers. BBB for short."

It was a great name.

Peter was the first guy who ever asked me to roller-skate with him. Maybe he's not that great of a writer, but boy, can he roller-skate. I don't mind his glasses.

"I—moved," he said.

"How come?"

Peter looked at his tennis shoes. "My parents got divorced. I live with my dad now. The new place is close to where he works."

A lot of my friends have divorced parents. It's no big deal around school. But I had never known anyone up close whose parents had decided to get divorced. So when it was my turn to say something back to Peter, I said something like: "Oh." It's hard enough talking to guys, let alone someone who just told you his parents got a divorce.

"Maybe I'll see you around school," he said, tossing a bag of M & Ms into the air and catching it.

"Yeah. Sure."

He headed for the checkout counter.

Chels caught up with me by the breakfast cereal. She was holding the stem of an acorn squash by two fingers.

"Who was that? That poet guy who asked you to skate? Did he ask you out or anything? What'd he say?"

"He said his parents got a divorce."

"I know tons of people who got divorced. It happens a lot." She waved her hand, as if to say, "So what?"

"Peter didn't look too thrilled about it."

"Of *course* he wasn't thrilled about it. No one is thrilled about it. But he'll get over it."

I wondered if *I'd* get over something like that if it ever happened to me. Probably not. But I take stuff like that very seriously.

# 3

We are having a jump rope unit in P.E. I am not
what is known as the athletic type, but it just so
happens that I am a pretty fair jump roper. For
once, I wasn't hating every minute of gym.

During my all-time record number of forward
jumps, Peggy Hiltshire came over to watch. She
had this crazy grin on her face. I tried to concen-
trate, but all I could see was Peggy and that grin.
Finally my nerves got the best of me. The rope
wound itself around my ankles, and I stopped. True
to form, Peggy didn't even notice that I found this
somewhat upsetting. Peggy is not the most obser-
vant person.

"Meet me at my locker after," she said, bouncing

19

from foot to foot. "I've got something *fabulous* to show you."

Peggy Hiltshire is one of those people who's always got something to show you. Once it was an old Missing-in-Action bracelet her older cousin had let her have. It had the name of a Vietnam vet on it, and the date he was last seen. The idea is that you wear the bracelet till the guy is found. It's a great idea, except that Peg gave me the impression she thought he'd someday come home and marry her. ("Oh, Peggy, dear, I saw your face in my dreams. It was all that kept me alive!") Peggy eats that stuff up. I didn't point out to her that, even if the guy were still alive, he'd probably be old enough to be her father.

Another time it was pictures of the horse her dad had bought. He was creamy brown with a thick, combed tail, and the prettiest eyelashes ever. He was beautiful. Peggy had about a hundred shots of him, but only a few were in focus.

So having Peggy want to show me something *fabulous* was not all that unusual. I knew from experience, however, that unless I said okay, she'd stand there bouncing around forever.

"Okay," I said.

She kicked her legs backward and yelled, "Yea!" Peg wants to be a cheerleader.

I went back to my forward jumps.

By the time I got to the locker room after gym, there was practically a meeting going on around

20

Peggy's locker. She'd invited a whole squad of people. I muscled my way in a little, enough to hear something about "romantic fires and snow a mile deep."

Miss Enod interrupted. "Excuse me. Ex-cuse me, lay-dies!" The group broke up. Have you ever noticed how nervous gym teachers get when people aren't taking their showers?

After that I only had about 4.5 minutes to get to my locker and then to science.

Chels was waiting by old 1132. "You hear Peggy's news?"

I shook my head, concentrating on my combination.

"Her parents have a condominium in Wisconsin. They're going on a skiing weekend over Christmas vacation. She gets to invite friends along."

I spun past the 15 and yanked up on the lever. It stuck.

"Did you hear me?" Chels demanded.

"Uh-huh. She was showing pictures in the locker room today, but I didn't see them."

"Vi-ic." She widened her eyes in exasperation. "Listen. You and me—we're invited."

We stood staring at each other. Finally I got my breath back. "Seriously?"

"She told me after humanities this morning. You ran out too fast. Only a few kids are invited." She looked at me. "Say something!"

"Seriously?" I said again.

21

She glanced up at the clock over our lockers. "You better get going—you're gonna be late. We'll talk about this after school. Meet me here!" She took off.

I slammed my door and made a dash for Mr. Stevenson's class around the corner, sliding into my back-row seat just as the bell rang.

"By the skin of your teeth, Mahoney," Mr. Stevenson said, lowering his eyebrows. He pretended to mark a big X in the attendance book with his red pen.

I like Mr. Stevenson. He talks tough, but he's actually pretty nice. And he seems to like me, but I don't know why. I'm not exactly a genius when it comes to chromosomes and stuff.

Fourth period is an extremely restless time. I think it's that just down the hall those lunch ladies are scooping tomato beef casserole into aluminum serving trays. Odors like that drifting around are bound to affect the brains of students all over the school.

"Today," said Mr. Stevenson, getting into his lecture pose, "let's talk about invertebrates."

"Let's not, " said Corey Talbott, who is also in my science class. The whole class laughed, except Mr. Stevenson.

Fourth period is full of rowdies. Corey Talbott is the worst. Today, for once, I tried not to notice him, but it's hard to ignore Corey and his friends. They drop their books. They poke the people ahead of them. They irritate the teacher. Today they had handfuls of swiped cafeteria straws. They were blowing the paper off them, seeing how many rows of tables they could shoot. For the hundredth time, I prayed a small thank-you that my seat was on the other side of the room.

Mr. Stevenson caught on, finally, and made Jerry Hansen pick all the wrappers up. This is just what Jerry wanted; at least that's how he made it look. He put on a real show. Then, when Mr. Stevenson turned back to the board, Corey tilted his chair back too far and fell backward.

Mr. Stevenson really let Corey have it. I have never seen him so mad. I could tell he was trying not to go overboard, because he had the same look my parents get when they're really upset: a little tight around the eyeballs.

After that, things were quieter. I was actually listening. "Invertebrates," I wrote carefully in my notes, "are well-adapted to their environments."

Then I got this creepy feeling, as though I were being watched. I looked up. The whole back row was staring at me. And a note was lying beside my open science book.

I slapped it between chapters two and three. Unlike some people, I'm not the type to put on a show for the whole fourth period.

My friend Melody McClure followed me to the lunchroom afterward. Melody's real name is Betsy Bonoff, but she started using Melody McClure as a

23

pen name in a writing class we both took last summer. She says it's more in keeping with her personality.

"Who's it from? Come on, Vickie, what's it say?"

I leaned up against the wall and unfolded the note.

*Corey Talbott dossn't like you. He loves you. From: someone who should no.*

"Whoever wrote it," I said, "can't spell."

"Let's see. Wow. *Loves* you. How romantic."

Ms. Runebach walked by just then with Mr. Dahl, the Health and Driver's Ed teacher. Those two have been getting pretty chummy lately, I've noticed.

"Vickie," she called. "Stop by my office after school today. Okay?"

"Right."

Ms. Runebach was my sixth-grade teacher, but she got promoted. She moved over to Keats to teach English. I never mind going to talk to her.

That afternoon she was sitting in her classroom, with her foot tucked under her. She looked like she was daydreaming, like a real person. I've always had this weird hang-up about teachers. Sometimes it's hard to imagine that they're people.

"If it isn't my favorite ex-pupil."

She always says that. I smiled back at her.

"I'm here," I said, dumbly. "I said I'd drop by."

"Yes, well, wait till you hear my news!"

I waited patiently in the chair next to hers while she dug around in her desk drawer. "Here it is," she announced. "Rules for the scholastic essay contest."

I'd never heard of it.

"Vickie," she said, leaning forward, "I want to enter you as one of the school's nominees in this essay contest. I'm only asking three people, and it's a nationwide test."

"Me? What do I have to do?"

"Write. It isn't until next fall, but you need to start working on your skills now. The Scholastic Committee comes up with a topic, and the entrants have one hour to write a brilliant essay. Your school record figures in, too, but that shouldn't be a problem for you."

That's what I like about Ms. Runebach. She is one of the most positive people I have ever met.

"It sounds great," I said.

"I was hoping you'd say that. Here's some added incentive: if you win first place, your prize is two hundred dollars." She put down the paper and crossed her arms smugly. "I think you can win."

The words were out of my mouth before I realized they were in my mind. "Oh, I'd never win."

"There you go again," said Ms. Runebach in a tired voice. But then she smiled. "Let's just wait and see, okay?"

She stuck her hand out suddenly. I shook it, embarrassed. Then she looked embarrassed. And we both laughed.

By the time I got back out to the hall, the place was practically deserted, which shows you how fast Keats clears out after the final bell. I didn't have to fight all those slamming bodies to get to my locker.

There was a folded note on 1132. For a second, I didn't even want to open it. Then I saw the handwriting. Chelsie's. "To Vic ONLY!" it said. "ONLY" was underlined three times.

*Where were you, anyway? I waited around for half an hour at least. Things to tell you. Call me.*
*C.*

It was nice walking home alone for once. Kind of a sweet-hurting, lonely feeling. The sun was out, but not full strength, and the colored leaves were damp, sticking to the bottom of my shoes. I like fall. But then, every time the season changes, I say I like *that* season best. I am very changeable, I guess, which in Minnesota is helpful. Dad says if you don't like the weather here, just wait ten minutes and it'll change.

All the way to Hancock Avenue, I thought about being nominated for the contest. Then I thought about winning the contest until I got to Loon Shore Drive. Then I stopped thinking about it. If you think about good things too much, you can ruin your chances to win. I know this is a very superstitious way to think, especially if you're a Christian. I should stop it.

There was a note for me on the kitchen counter, saying that Matthew, my five-year-old brother, was over at Blake's house. When did I get to be such a popular person to write notes to?

As I suspected, Mom and Dad were thrilled to pieces when they got home from work and heard my news. Parents make a very big deal out of things like scholastic essay contests.

"My daughter, the intellect." Dad was kidding, but I could tell he sort of meant it, too.

"I told you, I told you," Mom said, getting out glasses and plates and silverware for dinner. "You have talent. From here it's a short step to a full college scholarship."

Matthew, who had just gotten back from his friend's was suddenly interested. "If you won two hundred dollars, we could go to Disneyland." Disneyland is all Matthew thinks about these days.

"Forget it!" I snapped. Then I got a look at his face. "Two hundred's not enough for a trip to California. But it's enough to get a bike. One for you, one for me."

You'd have thought I'd given him the bike already, he gave me such a smile.

After dinner, I helped clean up. I usually do. Maybe that's part of being mature. I was excused, though, to go answer the telephone.

"It's always for you, anyway." Mom sighed. She loves to talk on the phone.

"This is your best friend, Chelsie Bixler. Remember me? Long hair? Braces? I'm the one who calls you every chance I get. I'm the one who hangs around your locker just to be nice. I'm the one—"

"Okay, okay. I'm sorry I didn't call. Something came up."

Immediately she was all ears. "Really? What?"

"I am one of Keats's three scholastic essay contest nominees."

"You're a *what*?!"

I explained about going into the classroom and Ms. Runebach sitting on one foot, and my saying yes I'll be in the contest.

"You're getting to be a very popular character, Vic. First Corey, now this. It's really great being friends with someone who's so popular."

I laughed. It was a nice idea, even if it wasn't exactly true.

# 4

I was lying on the bed watching Mom get ready for the party. Already she had tried on four different tops.

"All those women in crepe de chine dresses!" she moaned. "I'll never fit in."

Mom and I had been invited to a Merry Makeup Party at Mrs. Bixler's. It wasn't really a party. What would happen is a bunch of people would sit around in the living room while a Merry representative showed makeup samples. This is not Mom's idea of a good time.

"The last one I went to was a disaster," she said, struggling to button the sleeves of a white embroidered blouse. "The representative kept talking

29

about ways to camouflage my tiny undereye wrinkles. I didn't even know I had tiny undereye wrinkles. Now that's all I see when I look in the mirror."

"That skirt is nice, Mom."

"But it's denim," she moaned.

"It looks *good* on you."

"Then they drew names for a make-over, and I won. The woman *charged* at me, wielding an applicator. I've never seen so much green eye shadow in my life. When she got done I looked like a garter snake. Your father didn't want to let me in the house."

"If they pick your name for a make-over tonight, I'll take your place," I volunteered, buttoning the sleeve buttons for her.

"Big of you. Do you think it's too late to call in my regrets? I don't want to hurt Amanda's feelings. She thought I'd be *delighted* to come." Mom looked in the mirror. "What do you think of this top, Vickie? Does it make me look old? Do I look like the mother of a twelve-year-old?"

"It disguises your undereye wrinkles."

"Let's go. Before I change my mind."

Chelsie answered the door. "Come on in."

She looked nice in a pair of new pants. Suddenly my old jeans seemed *very* old. Decrepit.

Mom went into the living room to say polite things to the others.

30

"Where have you been?" Chels hissed at me. "I've been bored silly. Everyone keeps asking me how I like school." She rolled her eyes. "But the lady's going to do a Merry Makeup make-over later. Make a good impression and maybe you'll be chosen!"

Mom was very well behaved. She laughed at a bunch of silly makeup jokes and helped Mrs. Bixler pass cakes and pretty cookies. Chels and I were not so well behaved. We giggled a lot, until Mrs. Bixler gave us one of her looks. Then we tried harder to be mature.

The Merry representative wasn't so bad. She was wearing a blazer and a peach-colored corduroy skirt, not crepe de chine. She kept telling us to be the very best we could be. Then she showed us all kinds of diagrams—different layers of the skin and stuff. She told us all kinds of disgusting things about fatty deposits and clogged pores. I was beginning to feel sorry I had chowed down those cookies.

Finally she got out the makeup. Chels and I inched up on the edges of our seats. Up until last summer, I was hardly allowed to *touch* makeup. Finally my mom let me wear eye shadow—just a dab—and lipstick. Chelsie's parents held out until last month.

"Why don't we do a free makeover?" asked our Merry representative. "Let's see. How about a woman who has a birthday this month?"

Mom's birthday is the 13th! I flicked a look over

at her. She was sitting very still with a smile plastered on her face. She looked at me out of the corner of her eyes. *If you say anything, I'll kill you,* the look said, loud and clear.

I kept quiet.

"No one has a birthday?" Our Merry representative looked disappointed, like a teacher when no one can answer a very easy question.

A quiet lady in the corner raised her hand a little. "Mine's coming up in November," she offered, hopefully.

"Wonderful!" The woman started collecting utensils out of her carrying case—preparing for surgery. Chels heaved a great, letdown sigh.

All I can say is I'd never remember all the steps. I always thought you could just splash on some beige makeup. But before you can even start, you've got to analyze your skin type. Then there's cleansing formulas and something called astringent. Moisturizers go on top of that. *Then* you can put on foundation. But you've got to contour and stuff. I'd have to get up for school at least an hour earlier.

"—very inexpensive," said our representative, handing around order forms afterward. "Just check the box, and fill in the amount. I'll get you a total with my calculator."

She let us sample glosses and eye shadows and everything. She came over while Chelsie was putting on an eye shadow called Jade Moon. She used a swab to smooth it over Chelsie's eyelids, working it up to her brows. Chels looked in the mirror and smiled over at me. I didn't have the heart to tell her she looked like a garter snake.

To get my money's worth, I tried on as many eye shadow colors as possible. For a beginner I looked pretty good.

Mom was writing out a check. I took a look at her order form.

"Merry Nighttime Face Smoother and Daylight Skin Repair?" I asked, shooting my eyebrows into my forehead.

Mom wouldn't look at me. She kept writing. "I got something for you, too."

I checked.

"Mom! Baby Face Buffer?"

"Your voice is screechy. Don't get insulted."

"I can't believe it. Baby Face Buffer!"

"Sometime soon you may need it," she said, ripping out the check. "You'll thank me."

I hate it when Mom hints about stuff like that. It's an invasion of privacy. It's embarrassing.

After everyone left, Mom and I helped clean up. When he heard the rattle of dishes in the kitchen, Mr. Bixler came out of hiding. He must have been watching TV in the den.

"Is it over?" he asked, peering around.

"Yes, thank goodness," said Mrs. Bixler. Then she gave us an embarrassed look. "Those parties make me nervous. As if I'm supposed to care about my 'category of skin tone'! I only sponsored the

33

party because my friend Lucy pressured me into it."

Mom laughed. "I've never met anyone who really likes makeup parties."

Chelsie and I looked at each other. We sort of liked them.

"Really?" said Mrs. Bixler, beginning to smile, too. "I thought I was the only one."

"I despise them!"

Then we all broke up. Even Mr. Bixler.

Chelsie's mom made a tall stack of dishes by the sink, and then wiped her hands on a towel. "Well, I don't know about you, but I'm too keyed up to call it a night. And I don't feel like doing dishes. Do you all feel like a Coke or something at Dahlia's?"

"I'm game," Mom said.

Chels and I yelled out together: "Yeah!"

"Go ahead," said Mr. Bixler. "I'll hold down the fort."

Mrs. Bixler made Chelsie scrub all the Sunset Pink blush and Evening Eyes eye liner off her face before she'd let her go. She stood in the bathroom to make sure.

"Victoria," she said, "With just a touch less blush, your makeup would be perfect. My, that shadow certainly brings out your eyes."

I smiled at her. I could get to like Chelsie's mom.

"Move over," I said to Chels, who was dripping all over the sink.

At Dahlia's, Mom and Mrs. Bixler got a booth,

34

and Chels and I sat at the counter. The grill boy flipped burgers and sizzling hash browns. Then he came over to take our orders, and we both said coffee. The guy put down his pad and pencil and reached under the counter for cups and saucers. He slopped dark coffee into the cups and put them in front of us.

After I had taken a careful sip, I asked, "Did your mom buy you anything?"

Chels made a face. "Apricot Mask. Do I look like the type of person who needs Apricot Mask?"

No, she didn't. She had the greatest skin you've ever seen. I sighed. "My mom got me Baby Face Buffer."

"That's worse! Moms are a killer."

A bunch of guys slammed into the diner suddenly and started making a big scene. Worse than Chelsie, even. Without turning around, I recognized the voices.

"Russell Randolph," I said to Chels. "Paul Wong. Corey Talbott." They hang around together at school. You hardly ever see them apart. "They're all wearing the same kind of jeans and big T-shirts. Right?"

Chels giggled. "Right-o. They're cute, though."

I sighed and turned to look.

What a mess. Seventh-grade boys on the loose are not a pretty sight. They had taken over a booth, where they were bouncing around and laughing and spilling water.

35

The girls in the booth behind them were pretending not to notice, but they were talking awfully loud and shrieking once in a while, as if someone had pinched them. It made me sick.

When I was a kid, I decided something important. Before my hormones or whatever got out of control, I promised myself I'd never be one of those girls who giggles around boys. It's disgusting.

Chelsie worries me sometimes; I think she may be a potential giggler. I'd have to work extra hard this year to keep her in line.

I gulped a hot swallow of black coffee, and then poured in the cream.

"They're acting like real morons, aren't they?" Chels asked, making a face.

She understood. I grinned. We went back to business as usual.

"Hey, have you done any investigating about the mysterious love letters?" she asked, stirring a river of cream into her cup.

"Affirmative. But I don't have a thing to report. Yesterday I offered to collect assignments in Hartford's class, just to look at the handwriting. Nothing."

Chels sighed. "I haven't had much luck either."

"But I got another note. Did I tell you? Same handwriting. This one said he *loved* me. Can you believe it?"

"Love, huh? Sure, I believe it, in a way. I mean, it's not out of the question." She fastened a stern look on me. "Don't say it! I know what you're going to say! 'No one could ever possibly like me, Chelsie. I'm too homely. I'm too short. I'm too—'"

"*Chel*-sie!" I wish she wouldn't talk so loudly all the time. "Listen, it's not just me being too—too— whatever. It's him. We're nothing alike. We're in different cliques."

"Opposites attract," Chelsie said, narrowing her eyes significantly. "Take you and me."

Chels and I *are* different. She has bold green eyes. Chelsie's eyes say, "I'm not scared of anything." My eyes are kind of a wimpy brown. They don't say anything at all. And they *are* afraid. They're afraid of a lot.

Chels has exotic hair. That's the right word for it: exotic. It hasn't been cut since she was in second grade. I have brown hair. Quiet brown, like old brick. Chels and I are about as different as people can get.

We stayed a while longer, until we were floating in coffee, and until Corey and his friends got to be too much for Mom and Mrs. Bixler. Usually Chelsie and I are the noisy ones in a room. Not tonight.

Mrs. Bixler dropped us off. When she pulled into the driveway, the house looked like the most comfortable place in the world. Normally, it's really an ugly house. Really. My parents have big plans for it—but only *after* the important fix-ups. For instance, last fall we had to put in all new wiring.

Then we needed new copper water pipes. After that, attic insulation.

"Someday," Dad promises, "we'll paint, and this place'll look like the Taj Mahal. In the meantime, I guess we're stuck with an embarrassingly homely house."

Tonight a few hardy moths orbited the orange porch light, and the faint music of one of Dad's jazz records seeped into the yard. Bullrush looked down on us from my dark bedroom window, and the hall light made him glow like a jack-o'-lantern.

"See you tomorrow," said Chels, softly, while Mom and Mrs. Bixler were saying goodnight.

I waved, and then Mom and I walked to the front door together. I didn't speak, unwilling to break the mood of the magical house.

# 5

When I came downstairs later to say good night, Mom and Dad were talking quietly, but something about their tones made me stop. I stood in the hallway, not sure what to do next.

"You're being unreasonable," my mother's voice said above a swell in the record.

"And you're being childish," said my father's. Paper rustled. "Fifteen seventy-eight. You don't call that a foolish use of money? Where I come from, it's called extravagant."

Mom's voice was quiet. "I did it deliberately, Terry. Try to put yourself in my place."

"At least it could have been for something useful. But *cosmetics.*"

39

"I didn't want Vickie to feel left out. I would have been the only one who didn't order something."

Dad sighed an exasperated sigh.

"What I'm *trying* to say," Mom continued, "is that Vickie is at that age when—"

I took the stairs two at a time. The last thing I wanted to hear about was all the clogged pores I was going to get.

Bullrush was still sleeping on my bed. He greeted me with emerald-bright eyes. I closed the door and snapped off the light. It was cold up there, autumn cold. I huddled under the covers until I stopped shivering. Bullrush clawed at a soft spot in the covers purring, still part of that scene I had imagined when I had arrived home.

I am afraid of a lot of things. Bats, for one. One night last summer I woke up and there was one squeaking over my head. (Bats *squeak*. They have little mousy bodies and creepy Count Dracula wings, and they squeak out of their little voice boxes.) Dad had to come up with a butterfly net and catch it, and he was as scared as I was. Every time it flew over his head, he screamed and ducked. It took forever to catch that bat, because Dad kept ducking.

I'm also scared of things like strangers who are too friendly. Or of doing something completely stupid in front of other kids. But those fears were nothing compared to how I felt huddled in my bed that October night.

There was a soft knock at my door.

"It's Mom. May I come in?"

"Sure, Mom."

She switched my light on. "You're in bed early." Her face was scrubbed of the makeup. She looked okay. A little tired, but that's all.

Bullrush made a warm bed for himself on her lap and she stroked him patiently, avoiding the spot behind his ears that irritates him. I put my hands behind my head and hummed, trying to act natural.

"You okay, Vickie?"

"Sure I'm okay. I'm great. I'm perfect. Why wouldn't I be okay?"

"I thought you might still be mad at me about the Buffer."

"That was a great idea, that Buffer. That was probably the best idea you've ever had. I've been feeling the advance signs of minor facial breakouts. It's probably just a matter of time before acne sets in."

She gave me a strange look. "What'd you and Chelsie do tonight at Dahlia's?"

"Just drank coffee and stuff."

"Well, you're acting weird." She stroked Bullrush rhythmically without talking. Then, "Hey, why don't you pick me up after work tomorrow? You and Matthew. We can walk over to that produce market by the lake—the one that's selling pumpkins. 'Tis the season to pick out the world's greatest pumpkin, you know."

41

"We don't need a pumpkin, do we, Mom?"

"What's gotten into you? You don't want a pumpkin?"

"I was just sitting up here thinking that I could go without this year if I needed to."

"Why would you *need* to go without a pumpkin? My goodness. Are you leading up to me buying you something? New shoes, for instance?"

"No."

"A leotard? Remember that hot pink one you wanted last year? I'm glad I talked you out of that."

I shook my head.

"Boots!"

"I don't want anything."

Actually, at any instant of any day, there are one hundred million things I need to exist another second. But tonight, for once, I wasn't thinking about them.

"I guess I still believe in miracles," said Mom, shaking her head. "Well, even if *you're* not interested in pumpkins anymore, I'm willing to bet that Matthew *is*. Want to come along anyway and watch him go crazy?"

"Well, okay."

"I'm overwhelmed by your enthusiasm." She grinned at me, and the corners of her eyes tilted up and made me smile, too. But it wasn't an easy smile. It was a smile that felt like it had tears in it.

"Time for bed, okay? See you in the morning— bright and early." She deposited Bullrush back in a spineless lump on my bed and clunked downstairs in her clogs.

That night I kneeled down in the dark. I know there's no rule that says good praying happens on your knees, but sometimes it seems right.

"Dear God," my brain whispered. "God, I'm scared." I stopped and the sick feeling at hearing my parents argue came back. I shivered again. The hardwood floor felt cold and gritty under my bare feet.

Then I prayed silently:

"If it seems like I'm always coming to you when I have problems, it's because my life is *full* of them right now. Maybe you could do something about that. I would really appreciate it.

"In the meantime, take care of things with Mom and Dad. I'm really worried about them. I've hardly ever heard them argue like that. Remember how Peter's parents turned out. That would be terrible. I'll try to be more careful about money. Maybe that will help."

I felt a little better. When I finally crept back into my bed, the covers felt warm and heavy, the pillow cool and fresh smelling like laundry soap against my cheek. The folks were turning off lights on the second floor. The patch of warm light over my bed disappeared.

"'Night, Babe," Dad called softly up the stairs to me.

"Good night," I said.

43

# 6

By four thirty the next afternoon, my little
brother was ready to go pumpkin hunting.

The TV show I was watching was boring, but I
wasn't about to budge.

"Relax, Matthew. Mom doesn't get off until five.
We'd just end up waiting for her." I was very
logical—as logical as Dad is when he's explaining
why we can't stay up late.

"Vickie, we're going to miss all the good
pumpkins!"

"Read my lips, Matthew. Even if we go now,
Mom won't get off until—"

Matthew put his fingers in his ears and made the
face we call "Mr. Balloon."

I went to the closet to get our coats.

Willowood is about four blocks away, on the cleanest, neatest street you've ever seen. It's so clean there aren't even any trees, at least not any decent ones. The city planted some last summer, but they're so scrawny, I always feel like dropping each of them a fertilizer tablet. At least the trees in my neighborhood look as though they belong.

Outside Willowood, we passed up a lady in a wheelchair. I held the wheelchair access button for her, and she smiled a clear, happy smile. "Thank you, honey."

Matthew skipped inside.

Willowood Retirement Home smells like plastic—shiny, new plastic. The floor is so scrubbed you can practically see yourself in it. The aides are all scrubbed and bright, too, and they called out as I passed.

"Hi, Victoria. Haven't seen you in a while."

"How's seventh grade?"

No wonder Mom liked working here.

Matthew was heading straight for Mr. Smith's room, so I had to say excuse me to the aides and dash after him.

"It's me!" he was shouting through the door when I caught up.

"Howdy-ho!" Mr. Smith shouted.

We pushed open the door and went into the little room. Mr. Smith didn't rise out of his chair. But he lifted a hand in greeting.

"Didn't you bring your furry friend? Well, come in anyway. I'm wearing my teeth, and I don't want to waste the occasion."

Mr. Smith is a pet lover, but he doesn't own a cat or anything. Willowood won't let him. Every once in a while I cart Bullrush over for a visit. A bunch of Willowood folks voted him Mr. Congenial Cat awhile back.

Matthew climbed on the bed and made himself comfortable. "We're going to pick out a pumpkin," he announced. "With Mom."

"That so? Get a good one—ripe and orange. Not too skinny, either. Get a nice, round one."

"Ours'll be the best! With a corkscrew tail and no green spots."

"That's it, that's it!" said Mr. Smith. "You've got the makings of a real pumpkin connoisseur, Matthew."

"Right," agreed my brother, bouncing up and down on the bed.

"I was a pretty fair pumpkin picker in my day. Mother always let me choose the family pumpkin from Miz Averson's farm. My brother Herbert was a bully, and always wanted to pick. But she never let him. 'Course he always got dibs on the Christmas tree, the biggest piece of cake, the best store-bought shirt, and pretty near everything else. But not the pumpkin. No, sir. That was mine. I always got a humdinger, too."

Why did people like Mr. Smith have to get old?

46

It wasn't fair that he couldn't go out and find the greatest jack-o'-lantern in the state if he wanted to—just because he was old.

I had a great idea. "Want to come with us, Mr. Smith? I don't know where Ms. Averson's farm is, but I bet the produce stand we're going to will have pumpkins as good as you used to get."

Mr. Smith laughed till his shoulders shook.

"Ah, Victoria. Miz Averson is long gone, and her farm, too. There's a subdivision in its place—The Circle. Ever hear of it?"

"Sure! My friend Chelsie lives there. That used to be a farm?"

"Not so long ago, either. That's the trick with a lot of Minnesota suburbs. All agricultural, not too many years past."

"Well, do you want to come?"

"Thanks kindly for the offer. But these legs—I don't know. They're not used to long treks anymore. Probably couldn't make it."

"It's not far," said Matthew. "I walk there all the time."

"It's not far if you're five years old," said Mr. Smith, sighing. "Believe me, things change."

The mood in the room had gotten dark, like someone had pulled a shade. Even Matthew sensed it, and sat quietly on the bed looking at his hands.

Mr. Smith ran his hand over his sparse white hair and smiled feebly. "Wish I could go. It'd probably do me a world of good. Been feeling low, as of late.

If I don't snap out of it, I'll have to make a trip to see your mother." He laughed, but the dry chuckle didn't light his eyes.

I was staring at the window ledge. It was a nice, wide window ledge with plenty of room for a pumpkin. Why didn't the Willowood staff take care of it? People like Mr. Smith needed Halloween pumpkins.

He had some fresh licorice whips to share—red ones. We sat chewing and talking. Mr. Smith knows a lot of stuff about birds and classical music. He subscribes to all kinds of magazines. It was very interesting, but at five to five, I had to interrupt. It was time to pick up Mom. Matthew made a big fuss. Now he didn't want to leave. Brothers! I told him I'm go pick up Mom and swing by for him in a few minutes.

Mom's office is at the end of the hall. It's the door with the "B. Mahoney" plaque on it. The door was open a crack. Mom was inside, leaning her forehead against her hand. She looked tired.

"Mom?"

"Oh, Vickie. Is it finally five? Terrific. You saved my life. Where's Matthew?"

I pushed open the door. "We're picking him up at Mr. Smith's."

"How *is* Marvin?"

"Very depressed."

"I've noticed. He tries to put on like everything's okay, of course. He's always chipper as a bird when

48

I talk with him. But I get the feeling something's bothering him down deep. I'm glad you're a friend to him, Vickie. He's a lonely man."

"You okay, Mom?"

"Me? Oh, sure. It's been a wild day, but so what else is new?" She pushed back her chair and fished gloves out from the pocket of her old tweed coat. Then she put her arms through the sleeves. "Let's go pumpkin hunting!"

At the outdoor market I had the biggest and best pumpkin picked out before Mom and Matthew even got their bearings. I have pumpkin radar.

"No fair! I'm not done looking," Matthew said, taking off. "I want something weird!"

I picked up the pumpkin and cradled it like a baby. This was The Pumpkin, no question. It was heavy but I carried it around, trying to keep up with my mother and brother.

"Aren't these cute?" Mom asked, leading me to a display of baby pumpkins.

They were.

"Are they expensive?" she asked the man taking money.

"Not hardly! Two of these for the same price as a big one."

Then I had another great idea. "Mom?"

"Mmm?"

"Mr. Smith really likes pumpkins. Don't you think it's unfair that he doesn't have one?"

"I suppose," she said cautiously, raising an eyebrow. "It would probably be good for him."

"Right. So I was wondering. Could we get two little pumpkins instead of a big one? We could carve one for us and one for Mr. Smith."

Mom's mouth dropped open. "Is this Victoria Hope Mahoney, my daughter, the *princess* of huge pumpkins?"

"If you'd *heard* him, Mom."

"I think," she said, "that's one of the nicest ideas you've ever had. Let's see what Matthew says."

Will wonders never cease—that's what my dad would have said if he'd been there to hear Matthew. Mom and I went over to talk very seriously with him about this pumpkin issue. But before we could even open our mouths he was carrying on about none of the pumpkins were weird enough and the one I had picked out was no good and he wished he could find something really great—

"Vickie and I have an idea—" Mom said, giving me a sly look.

At home, Matthew drew a face on his pumpkin, and Mom carved it. It was scary. It had slanty eyes and shark teeth. Sometimes I think there's something wrong with Matthew—all those cartoons have demented him.

The pumpkin I carved had u-shaped eyes, no teeth at all, and a pug nose.

"It looks like Mr. Smith," said Matthew approvingly. "When he's not wearing his dentures."

50

"That," said Dad, "is a benign jack-o'-lantern."

"A *therapeutic* jack-o'-lantern," Mom corrected. She was pleased. I could tell.

"I wouldn't have the heart to make that one into a Prize Terry Mahoney Pumpkin Pie," said Dad. "He's too nice. *This* one, however"—he turned, snarling and extending clawlike fingers at Matthew's pumpkin—"is doomed."

Matthew shrieked happily. Then he carried his pumpkin out to the coffee table so it could sit in the window.

Later that night, Dad and I delivered my pumpkin to Willowood. We even took a candle and some matches. The night nurses and aides grinned at us as we passed. Jolly the jack-o'-lantern grinned back.

# 7

"Are you going on Peggy's skiing weekend?"

It was Monday morning, and Hilary Clifford was yelling over from her locker across the hall. Usually Hilary doesn't even talk to me, something I have gotten used to in junior high. Some people are normal, and some people act as though they don't even *see* you.

"I—I don't know," I stammered back. *Wow, Vic. Intelligent.*

"She invited you, didn't she?"

"A friend told me about it. I heard it through the grapevine."

Hilary walked over. "What friend?"

"Chelsie Bixler."

"She's invited, too?" Hilary chewed on that for a second. "I'm going. I don't like skiing that much, but I've got to get out of the house over Christmas break. Wouldn't you just die to get away from your parents?"

I tried to get my tongue working again. My jaw was stuck, like the Tin Man's in *The Wizard of Oz*.

She looked at me closely. "Aren't you in my science class?"

"I don't think so. I'm in fourth period."

"Oh, really? Well . . . see you around."

Her shoulder-length hair swung as she walked slowly away. *I'll bet*, I thought, as I fiddled with my padlock, *I'll just bet that Hilary Clifford's locker combination never sticks.* I rummaged around in my messy locker, trying to find my math book.

"Hey, Mahoney!"

Peter! He was smiling like crazy. He'd never called me Mahoney before.

"Catch!" he shouted, dropping a wadded paper and doing some fancy soccer moves—bouncing it around his leg, and finally doing a great side kick to me. Then he laughed and disappeared down the hall.

I unwadded the paper. Of course there was nothing inside. *Boy, Mahoney,* I thought, *talk about wishful thinking. Do you think everyone's dying to write notes to you?*

Mrs. Hartford was her usual self. Boring. I

daydreamed. I thought about skiing weekends and parent problems and the cat show.

"Rarely," Mrs. Hartford announced, "have I seen a classroom full of such dull faces. And I've been teaching for seventeen years."

She should try being a student in one of her own classes, for once. Especially in the middle of October when the newness of school has just worn off.

She turned to pull the hall door shut. At the same instant, a note came flying over my shoulder.

Mrs. Hartford is quick, I'll say that for her. She turned just in time to find the whole class staring at me.

"Ms. Mahoney, you seem to be the center of everyone's attention. Care to share your secret with the rest of the class?"

"No, thanks," I said. "Ma'am." I was very cool, considering I was scared spitless.

"What's that? A note? Victoria Mahoney. You *know* how I feel about notes."

I wanted to yell, "Well, *I* didn't write it!" But, I didn't, of course. Only people like Hilary Clifford or Peggy Hiltshire or Chelsie Bixler would have the guts to do something like that.

"Since you're so intent on disrupting class, let's hear what it says."

Some teachers have no sense. I could have told her that reading a note out loud was the dumbest thing she could do, but I don't think she was interested in what I thought. She plowed right in.

" 'He's dying of love for you, Vickie," she read.
" 'Why don't you at least talk to him?' "

My ears went hot. My knuckles went cold.

Mrs. Hartford waited for the laughter to settle. "It's unsigned. And the spelling is atrocious. All right, I want to know who passed this note to Vickie."

She waited for a good two minutes, but no one confessed. Mrs. Hartford looked as though she might pressure cook before our eyes. "I'm letting it go—this time," she said finally, twisting her earring 160 dgrees. "But if there's any more trouble, the consequences will be dire. Do you hear me? Dire!"

Whatever that meant.

Mrs. Hartford rapped her knuckles on her desk top. "From now on I want your full attention. I hope you've all learned a lesson."

There was snickering in the back row, right side.

"That goes for you, too, Mr. Talbott!"

# 8

"SHE DID *WHAT?*"

Good old Chelsie. She was the one person madder at Mrs. Hartford than I was.

She walked me to P.E., and the more I told her, the louder she got.

"There's something wrong with her. That was just plain mean."

Behind us, Hilary was walking old Peg to P.E. When Peggy caught a whiff of trouble, she came bouncing up.

"Howdy, girls," she sang in her Mississippi accent. "What's going on?"

"You won't believe this, Peggy," Chels started, and then the story was out.

Peggy was furious. She waved her arms around and called Mrs. Hartford an old bag. Chels said we should try to have her kicked out of school. I don't know what Hilary thought. She just stood there with her arms around her books.

I was glad everyone was mad at Mrs. Hartford. I only felt a little guilty. I suppose Jesus would have forgiven Mrs. Hartford. But she had been mean! She had been unfair!

In the locker room, Peggy had her ski resort brochures handy. I flipped through them. There were a lot of pictures of snow, lifts, and skiis crossed over fireplaces. Also shots of laughing people sitting around tables wearing ski caps.

"That's the lodge," Peggy explained. "We'll probably go there for meals and stuff. Mom said she's not spending her vacation cooking. You're coming, aren't you? I can only ask three people, and Charita and Susie can't go. That leaves Chelsie and you."

*Real tactful, Peggy,* I thought. But I didn't care if I was first choice or not—the pictures had done it. My mouth was practically watering.

"I'll ask," I said. "Tonight."

Peggy squealed and squeezed my arm.

But later I changed my mind. It's a long story, but it started when Dad got home that night . . . finally. He'd been working an awful lot of overtime at the restaurant lately.

57

"Matthew," he said, without even saying hi or anything, "how many times do I have to tell you to park your bike inside the garage instead of in the middle of the driveway?"

Matthew must have heard something unusual in Dad's voice, too. He scrambled up from his spot in front of the TV like a flash. It was amazing.

"Well, it's too late now. I already moved it."

"Sorry, Dad," said Matthew sorrowfully, standing there like a rabbit frozen in someone's headlights.

Dad pulled out a kitchen chair and sat down. He didn't say anything else.

We sat down for a late dinner. Mom prayed.

"Dear Father, we always appreciate your help. But now more than ever be with our family. Thanks for loving us. Your love is bigger than any problem. Amen."

Some prayer.

I put it out of my mind, concentrating instead on my plans. I rehearsed all through dinner: "Peggy's parents have invited me and two other well-mannered girls on a skiing weekend. They will be the chaperones. You can't watch after seventh-grade girls too closely, ha-ha."

Then I realized what was weird about dinner tonight. No one was talking.

I picked the nuts carefully out of my cake, postponing my plans to mention skiing—at least until our family was on speaking terms again.

# 9

Around the end of October I usually start thinking about ways to scare my brother. Last year, for instance, I tied a rope from his doorknob to the bathroom's and then I made spooky noises. Matthew couldn't get out of his room and he yelled his head off. It was a very mean thing to do, and I got in plenty of trouble. This year, however, my mind was too full of other things.

I was sure of it now. My parents were having problems.

I only remember one other fight between Mom and Dad. It was a couple of years ago, and it was a humdinger.

Dad wanted to invite his cousin's family from

59

Stillwater over. Mom was very calm. She said they were the rudest people she'd ever met in her life. Dad said we owed them a dinner. Mom said they were rude, rude, rude. So rude they didn't deserve dinner—at our house or anywhere else.

Dad cooked a huge dinner—the works. Dad's cousin kept sniffing and talking about "cat smell." His wife's name was Evelyn. She had a cholesterol problem. She told us the details over Dad's potato soup, such as she had to watch out for heavy foods. Even their little kid was rude. He kept kicking me under the table.

Mom was furious about the whole visit. After the company left, she and Dad argued in loud, angry voices—for an hour at least.

But this wasn't like the Stillwater cousin fight. It felt different. Something was wrong. I knew it.

It was an emergency.

I found Peter's address in the phone book. He lived only a couple of blocks away. I walked over on a sunny Saturday morning. His house reminded me of ours—it needed a good coat of paint.

I rang the bell.

The man who came to the door smiled through a thick, bristly moustache and opened the screen door. He was wearing Levis and a flannel shirt. It had to be Peter's dad. So that's what a divorced man looked like.

"Hello," he said, pleasantly. "Girl Scout cookies? Newspaper collections? UNICEF?"

60

"N-no. Is . . . um . . . Peter home?"

His smile widened. "Sure, he's home. Come on in. Peter!" he called. "Girl here to see you!

How embarrassing. I almost died.

Then Peter showed up. He looked good in straight leg jeans and a red sweat shirt. "Hi," he said, squinting at me.

"Hi. It's Victoria." (Pause here for Victoria to roll her eyes. What a dumb thing to say!)

He laughed. "I know it's you, Vickie!"

"You were squinting. I thought maybe you didn't recognize me."

"Contacts," he said. "Just got 'em."

We looked at each other.

"Look," I said, finally, "can I talk to you for a second? I sort of have something important to ask you about."

"Dad!" Peter called. "I'm going outside, okay?"

"Sure thing!" I could tell his dad was trying not to laugh. How embarrassing.

We walked toward the lake, not to be romantic or anything, but to get out of the neighborhood. I think we were both worried that anyone from school would see us and think something weird. In junior high you have a lot of strange things you have to worry about.

"What's up?" he asked. He didn't seem nervous at all. I was. Boy, was I nervous.

"It's about my parents."

I said it in a rush. "I need to know the advance

signs of divorce. My parents are acting pretty strange."

"Do they fight a lot?"

"They don't really fight, but every once in a while they talk loudly at each other. You know. It's not really arguing; it's more like discussing things tensely. My parents are very civilized."

"Yeah. So were mine."

It was the "were" that got me. It shut me up for a while.

"I'll tell you what to look out for. *Not* talking. It's when parents stop talking that you know you're in trouble. Right before they told me they were separating, Mom and Dad stopped talking to each other. And my father hardly even came *home* at night. He worked over all the time."

I swallowed.

"And things weren't even that busy at work. Now he comes home early a lot."

I had hoped Peter could cheer me up. But I had been wrong. I felt like I'd gotten kicked in the stomach. With boots. With hiking boots from Colorado.

"That's all I needed to know," I said.

"Sorry," said Peter with a sigh, "I'm not much help. What are you going to do?"

I was asking *him!* I only knew one thing I could do, and that was to pray. So I did. Silently, while Peter stood there, scuffing twigs with his shoes. And it sounded a lot like the prayer I had heard

Mom pray a couple nights ago. *I need your help, God.*

"Well, thanks anyway, Peter. I figured you'd be the guy to ask."

"Yeah," he said. "I know all about divorce. That's why I took that writing class last summer—to get out of the house. It was too depressing at home."

"I'm sorry. I didn't know that." If I had known, at least I could have said something comforting. Something like "Hang in there," or "Don't give up, Peter, old guy."

"It's okay," said Peter. "Things are okay, now. Not the same, but okay. . . . Look, this conversation is depressing. Want to do something?"

"Sure. What?"

"Canoe?"

"I'm a superb canoer. Dad taught me. But I only canoe with a life preserver."

"We have life preservers—and a canoe. I'll ask Dad to help us carry it down to the lake."

Following Peter back to his house, I wondered if this could be considered a date. I'd ask Chelsie. She'd know for sure.

# 10

My arms were aching, but I felt pretty good walking home a couple hours later. I am a very good canoer, due to Dad's excellent teaching skills.

When I got to the house, Chels was lying on her back in our front lawn. I blinked a couple of times before I figured out that it was Bullrush curled in a sleeping ball on her stomach.

"What are you doing?" I yelled at her over the fence.

"Resting," she said, without opening her eyes. "Cats and human beings find this a relaxing way to spend an autumn afternoon."

I walked to the gate and opened the latch.

Chels cracked one eye open. "Where have *you*

been? I've been here for half an hour. Your mom said she didn't know where you went. She didn't sound all that happy about it."

"You'll never believe it."

"Try me."

"Peter's."

"You're kidding." Chels sat up, but gently so as not to disrupt Bullrush. "Did he invite you?"

"No. I went over myself."

"That's almost better. Proves you have guts. How come you went over there? Are you in love or something?"

"No!" I said, blushing without wanting to. "I had something to ask him about."

"Like what?"

I didn't feel like talking about my parents, so I told her about the canoeing instead.

"What are *you* doing here?" I asked.

"Well, in case you've forgotten, a certain important event is coming up fast. A certain cat show. Did you, by any chance, forget about the cat show next weekend?"

"Of course not."

"I came over to inspect our entry, and just look at him! You call that a shiny coat?"

"He's gorgeous! A prime speciman. Every day I give him a teaspoon of cod liver oil. Not to mention the time he knocked the bottle over and drank half of it before I got it away from him."

"He doesn't look all that shiny to me. At this

rate, maybe you should *dip* him in cod liver oil instead of feeding it to him."

"Ha-ha."

"And look at his toe pads. They're calloused!"

"He's a busy cat."

"There's gunk in his eyes. Vic, if you're not going to take this show seriously, I'll have to. Bullrush's condition calls for drastic measures."

"Like what?"

I followed her to the bathroom. She unloaded practically the whole medicine cabinet. Gently she swabbed the top pink insides of his ears. She rubbed Vaseline into his toe pads. She tissued the sleep out of his eyes. Bullrush looked as though he was hating every minute of it.

"Now for the tour de force!"

"The tour of what?"

"The final step. The bath!"

Chelsie had never given Bullrush a bath. If she ever had, she'd never have suggested we try it, especially without some sumo wrestlers to pin him in the bathtub.

"I was kind of hoping we could skip that part."

"Are you *kidding?* This is the most important thing! We wouldn't even get through the show gates if we didn't give the cat a bath!"

I started to explain about extreme cat panic, but Chels wasn't listening. She was digging in the linen closet.

"You got an old towel we can use to dry him?

And one to put on the bottom of the bathtub so he doesn't slide around?"

It was useless to argue.

I found a couple of torn terrycloth towels that have been around as long as I have. Chelsie spread one neatly in the bathtub; then she turned on the water, full blast.

"Don't worry, Bullrush," she crooned. "Everything's in control."

Bullrush already knew things were in control. *His* control. I felt the pinpricks of his toenails curling through my jeans.

"Okay," said Chels, tucking her hair behind her ears and twisting off the nozzles. "That should do it. Upsy-daisy." She pulled Bullrush off my lap. His claws came out of the denim with little snaps.

There was a blur of cat limbs and a spray of water.

"I told you! I told you!" I shouted.

Chels dropped Bullrush. He bounced out of the bathtub like a wet panther and headed for the door. Luckily, I had thought to close it. He turned on his muscular legs. Water flew everywhere. He jumped onto the toilet seat. Sprang onto the tank. Hopped into the sink. Made a wild leap and landed back in the tub. Chels got a tight, stunned grip on him.

"Wow," she said. "Maybe you were right."

I handed her the shampoo.

# 11

When we finished, Bullrush was mad but gorgeous. Chelsie took a Polaroid. It didn't turn out because Bullrush was glaring at the camera. He wouldn't even purr for three straight hours, which is practically a world record for him. I thought we had damaged his personality or something. But finally I got the purring to start up again, like the motor of an old lawn mower. Amazing what a few liver snacks can do.

The cat show cage decorations were my idea. We painted a poster that looked like stage scenery, with trees on either side and some black hills far away. Behind the hills we wrote: BEHOLD, THE STAR!

We made stage curtains from blue velvet scraps

and gold fringe—Chels pinned and I sewed. I couldn't get the seams straight on Mom's old sewing machine. Then Chelsie made me laugh and I almost sewed right over my finger.

We planned to hang the curtains at the front of the cage and have Bullrush lie inside like a celebrity. It'd be great. Chelsie wanted to rig up stage lights—little round ones that would look like real footlights—but I voted them down. I was afraid they'd singe his whiskers.

Everything took a lot longer than we expected, and we were getting hungry. I dubbed Chels supper guest of the evening; then I had a double inspiration.

"Let's invite Peggy over! That way my parents can see what a great person she is. Sort of get them used to the idea of our Christmas trip."

"Vic, sometimes your ideas border on brilliant."

I'll say one thing for my parents. No matter what, they are always, *always* generous.

I brought it up with Dad, who had the night off from the restaurant. "Sure thing," he said. "Ask your little friend over. I've been dying to meet this Peggy person."

*Little friend?* I got this sickening feeling that the Third Degree was coming for poor old Peg. Every time my parents meet a new kid I hang around with we go through the Third Degree. I hoped Peggy wouldn't do anything weird, like squeal about her sort-of boyfriend, Al Rodrieguez. My parents are not at all ready for boyfriends and stuff yet.

"Hi, Peg," I said, opening the door when she rang. "You look great." She did. She was wearing great new jeans and a very normal sweater. She looked like the kind of friend every parent dreams about. I led her into the kitchen.

"Hi, you guys. Hello, Mr. and Mrs. Mahoney. It was really nice of you to invite me over."

My dad was grinning, a good sign.

"What took you so long?" Chels asked. "We were getting ready to eat without you, for Pete's sake."

Peg sighed a huge, exasperated sigh. "I would have been here sooner, but Daddy made me change. I had on this *fantastic* outfit: this T-shirt that has a picture of a big ole monkey on it, and on the back it says, 'I'm an Animal.' It's hysterical!"

I didn't look at Mom and Dad, but I knew they were giving each other Looks. That's Looks with a capital L.

At dinner Dad teased Chelsie about her brilliant acting career at Keats, and Mom wanted to hear all about the cat show decorations. They were acting like themselves. I was glad I hadn't said anything to Chelsie about the divorce. *Boy,* I thought, *I sure do have a vivid imagination. No wonder Ms. Runebach thinks I'm creative.*

Matthew kept staring at Peg; I could see the question forming in his little brain. Finally he came out with it.

70

"How come you talk that way?"

I caught Chelsie's attention. *Here we go*, my eyes said.

*You can say that again*, hers said back.

Peg laughed a bird laugh. "I'm from Mississippi, silly!" she said, cheerful as anything.

She started ranting and raving about Mississippi. Jazz this and barbecue that. Then Dad said he once had been to a Creole cooking seminar in Louisiana. I started to get the feeling that the whole evening might work out after all. Yes, sir, I could already feel the spray of powder in my face and the grip of poles in my mittens. *Wisconsin*, I thought, with a happy smile, *here I come*.

# 12

Corey was acting like a real goon. He had made a pair of floppy rabbit ears out of paper, and whenever Mrs. Hartford turned toward the board he stuck them on top of his head. They must have had some kind of tape on them, because they stayed up there, flapping around.

"If the sum of A and 25 is equal to or less than A times B plus C—" droned Mrs. Hartford, her chalk tapping out a beat on the board.

Corey waved his ears gracefully.

"—here's how we find the value of A."

Corey held his hands near his chin, like paws. He wriggled his rabbity nose.

"This same formula works in a variety of equations. May I have a volunteer to—?" Mrs. Hartford whirled around suddenly and caught Corey, ears and all, chewing an imaginary carrot.

"That's it!" she said, throwing down the chalk. "Get out of this room at once, Corey Talbott! Down to the principal's office. Now." She stalked back to his desk and yanked the ears out of his hair.

Corey yelled loudly when the tape came loose. It was a good act. The laughter we had been holding in came choking out.

"Quiet!" she said, scanning our faces as she crumpled the paper ears. She took a breath, and her skin faded to a calmer pink. "I want you to know why I'm sending Corey to the principal's office. Number one, I'm sick and tired—"

There was more, of course, but no one was listening. We were watching Corey hip-hop toward the door. He turned to look coyly at us over his shoulder. I clapped a hand over my mouth to stop the laughter.

"Victoria Mahoney!"

I jumped.

"I didn't do anything," I said.

"Get out of here!" said Mrs. Hartford, pointing. "I will not tolerate this kind of disturbance in my classroom."

"But, Mrs. Hartford—"

"Out!"

In seconds, I was out the door, heading toward Ms. Elk's office. It was incredible. In my whole entire life, I'd never been sent to the principal's office.

Corey led the way, walking as though he looked forward to getting there. I couldn't believe it.

Corey didn't hold the door open, but he gave it an extra wide swing so I could slip in behind him. He went up to the counter.

"Mrs. Hartford sent us," he told the secretary.

We were nodded into chairs.

"Ever done this before?" Corey asked me, chewing gum.

"No."

"Don't worry. Nothing to it. You'll be back on the streets in no time." He laughed at his own private joke while I stared at him.

Maybe the notes had been true. Maybe Corey Talbott liked me—a little. I mean, why was he talking to me?

Mrs. Hartford strode in, her skirt swaying. She went into the principal's office. When she came out, she gave us both angry looks and left.

I felt sick to my stomach.

Ms. Elk, the principal, has a terrible reputation. *Now I find out for myself*, I thought when she called us in.

I'll say this: Her voice *is* scary. It's deep. She asked what happened, and I told her I hadn't done *anything*, just laughed at Corey with everyone else. She acted as though she believed me. And she was actually quite interested in Corey's ears.

"Very inventive, Corey, very. But why? You told me last time you were in here that you would try to shape up."

Corey shrugged.

While we sat there Ms. Elk called up Corey's mom. She set up a meeting in her office with Corey and his parents the next morning before school. Corey looked over at me and smiled crookedly. Then Ms. Elk said she was writing a note to my parents telling them I had been to her office.

"Take a seat out in the lobby until the bell," Ms. Elk said, standing. "I hope this is the last I see the two of you here. Really. Make an effort."

Corey stretched out his legs and leaned back in the uncomfortable plastic chair, his back to the big glass window behind us.

"This is the life!" he said.

I smiled at him. Just to be polite.

"Hey, you learning anything in that Hartford class?" he asked. "I'm not. I hate that class. It's boring."

"It is boring, but I've learned some stuff."

I have this thing about school. I have to get good grades. At least I have to try to get good grades. So even if I hate the class, I do my best.

"But it's boring all right," I repeated.

"You really got in trouble the other day," he said, grinning again. "That was a weird note."

I broke into a sweat. What if Corey figured out who the note had been about! I would die.

"Yeah. I'm not sure what it was all about, exactly." I looked at my feet. "I don't even know who started it."

"Jennifer Meyerhauser. I saw her."

*Jennifer!*

The bell rang. I was still trying to digest the new information. Peg and Hilary were in the hallway, gawking at me and Corey. Peg waved like a crazy person, but Hilary looked stunned. Her mouth was open. They walked past.

Ms. Runebach came striding by, too, in her pretty plain skirt and flat shoes, pushing back her wavy, dark hair. When she got a look at me, her smile turned into a concerned line. That's when I jumped up, grabbing my books.

"Gotta go!" I said, reaching for the door. I left Corey in the dust.

# 13

Ms. Elk's secretary must be the fastest typist in North America. The letter came two days later.

"What's this?" said Mom, squinting and holding the envelope to the light. "It's not report card time."

"I've been meaning to tell you something, Mom—"

I *had* meant to tell. But Mom had been tired. Dad had been grumpy. I figured that news about my trip to Ms. Elk's would just add to the problems, whatever they were. Now it was all coming out anyway—all because of old Mrs. Hartford. I hated her!

Sullenly, I watched Mom read. She finished the

letter once, and started over. Finally she looked over at me, slumped into a chair.

"You were sent to the principal's office?" she asked in a dangerous voice.

"But it was a mistake," I explained. "Mrs. Hartford hates me! I didn't do anything, Mom. Honest."

"Hmm." She pushed back her hair and took a breath. She was struggling to stay under control. Finally she looked at me and said. "Okay. If you say so, I believe you."

"Thanks, Mom." I was so grateful I didn't know what else to say.

"I trust your word because you've always tried to be honest with me in the past. But why didn't you tell me about this yourself?" The dark tone was back.

"I—I don't know," I said. "I just couldn't."

"Victoria," Mom said, putting the letter down on the table and going to get a cup of coffee. "I'm your mother. You're supposed to tell me things like this. Have I ever been unreasonable? Have I ever blamed you for something that wasn't your fault?"

Probably she had, but I couldn't think of any specifics. So I said, "No, I guess not."

Mom sat down at the table with me. "Then you shouldn't be afraid to tell me about things like being sent to Ms. Elk's office."

I picked up the letter. "... *no further disciplinary action,*" said the heavy, black typewriting, *"unless there is a recurrence. . . ."* It sounded like a description of a criminal.

"Hi, honeys," said Dad coming into the kitchen. He took a look at our faces. "What?"

Mom handed him the letter. "The principal at Keats sent this letter, but Vickie says she didn't do anything to warrant it. I believe her."

Dad read silently. "Why didn't you tell us about this?"

What do parents do, rehearse ahead?

"I wanted to, but—" I said, trailing off. What would they say if I told them it was because of *them* that I hadn't told?

Dad pulled up a chair and put his hand over mine (a good sign). "This is a serious matter, Vickie. Parents have this strange hang-up: They like to help their kids."

"If we'd known," Mom added, "we could have gone to talk to this Mrs. Hartford." She looked over at Dad. "Do you think it's too late to speak with her?"

"Arggghh!" I groaned, yanking my hand away from Dad. "You can't! You positively can't! It would ruin me. Mrs. Hartford hates me as it is."

Dad stroked his chin. "Now wait a minute. If you didn't do anything, why does she hate you?"

I hesitated. I had a sudden feeling that I was heading for trouble.

"The whole situation doesn't seem very plausible to me. Does it to you, Bob? From a purely psychoanalytical point of view?"

"Not in the least. I get the feeling there's something we don't know about. Is there, Vickie?"

"Oh, all right."

I told them everything. About the notes and Corey and the rabbit ears. They listened politely. Dad continued to stroke his chin, and Mom twisted a strand of hair around her finger and looked thoughtful. When I finished, I was sort of relieved. I'd been worried about the notes and stuff for a long time.

Dad heaved a great sigh. "*Now* I understand. It explains a lot."

"Well?" I said.

"Well, what?"

"You're the parents. Give me some terrific advice."

"Well," said Mom, resting her ankle across her knee and fiddling with the fringe on her loafer, "I'll tell you what I'd do in the same situation."

"What?"

"Confront this Jennifer Meyerwhatever. She's the one who's been getting you into trouble. Wouldn't you like to find out why?"

Not if it meant talking to Jennifer. She is not exactly my type. She's one of Peggy's strange friends who thinks heaven on earth is being named part of the seventh-grade cheerleading squad.

"It wouldn't hurt to talk to your teacher," said Dad. "Don't forget that as a Christian you should show this Mrs. Hartford a little forgiveness. And it seems you might owe her an apology, too. You *did* laugh."

I said I'd think about it . . . but I definitely wasn't excited about the idea.

"Is this family crisis solved?" Dad stood up and stretched. "If so, I can start dinner."

"My daughter, the juvenile delinquent," Mom moaned. "What next?" She cocked an eyebrow at me. "You're not going to turn into one of those unmanageable teenagers, are you, Victoria? Because I don't think I could handle it. I really don't."

I sensed that the storm had passed. Actually, they'd been pretty decent about everything. I wondered how Mr. and Mrs. Talbott had reacted in Ms. Elk's office.

"Don't worry, Mom. I won't even *be* a teenager for ten more months."

"Probably the day you turn thirteen you'll want a Princess phone installed in your room. And your own MasterCard, right? So you can charge outlandish clothes."

"And a Harley-Davidson, of course," I added. "To get around town."

"And you'll stop eating your father's good cooking and demand fast food at every meal. And when people ask, 'How are your parents these days, Victoria?' you'll say, 'Those old bats! Who cares?'"

"I'm feeling the twinges already!" I said, throwing my arms out dramatically.

"I just had a terrible thought," Dad interrupted darkly from the kitchen.

We both turned to look at him.

"Matthew will be thirteen in eight years. We'll have to go through this teenage stage all over again."

Mom and I both groaned.

# 14

"Wow," exclaimed Chelsie, with bugged-out eyes. "Everywhere you look, cats."

The assembly hall was crawling with them. Rows and rows of cages on rows and rows of tables. And tons of owners, carrying combed and purring cats around in their arms. *Bullrush,* I thought happily, *is the most gorgeous cat in the place*.

"Let's find our cage," Chels said, weaving up and down the aisles. "Our entry number is seventy-one. Seventy-one, seventy-one. Where is it?"

The curtains and the scenery looked pretty good, and a lot of the other owners came by to gawk. Almost everyone was friendly, even considering Bullrush was by far the most qualified cat there. He sprawled calmly inside the cage, beefcake-style. He knew he was a winner.

The judging started, and we went to sit by the ring.

"I want a cat like that," Chels whispered during the judging of the Blue Persians. "They really are blue! On second thought, I'll have one of those." She laughed and pointed out a Manx, a tailless kind of cat that looked like a rabbit from behind.

Two seats down, this old guy was staring at me. He was sitting back in his chair with his hands folded over his comfortably large stomach, smiling. I nudged Chelsie.

"That's Grandma Warden's friend," she whispered. "Remember? Mr. Wilkes!"

I felt guilty right away. At Grandma Warden's funeral last summer, we had promised to visit him. I hoped he wouldn't try to talk to us. Maybe we could sneak out without his noticing.

But Mr. Wilkes slid down next to Chels.

"Hi, girls! Fancy meeting you here. You're Chelsie Bixler. And Victoria Mahoney. Right?"

"Right," said Chels. "Hi, Mr. Wilkes. What are you doing here? Did you enter your cat?"

"Nooo," he said, pronouncing it "newwww." "Just came to watch. Used to own prize-winning Abyssinians, though. Guess cat shows are in my blood. How about you two? Bring a couple of fancy felines for show?"

Mr. Wilkes, I noticed, only talked in partial

84

sentences. It was a strange, familiar way of talking. I liked it.

"Vic, here, did. She has a super-beautiful cat named Bullrush. We entered him in the Household Pet division."

"Well, let's see him!" said Mr. Wilkes.

We abandoned our seats to go catch a peek of Bullrush. Mr. Wilkes agreed that he was a fine, royal animal.

"No skin and bones on that cat!" Mr. Wilkes crowed, slapping his own hip.

"He's not fat," I said.

"At least not too fat for a snack. They had complimentary cans of food in back. Let's get Bullrush a little treat. Come with me."

At noon we put a padlock on Bullrush's cage, and Mr. Wilkes escorted us to a tiny restaurant a few blocks away. He bought us each a tomato, cheese, and sprouts sandwich, plus mineral waters. The meal was extremely healthy. My mother would have been thrilled. The great thing was, it tasted delicious.

"Yes, sir. Being here brings back my cat-showing days. Makes me wish I could keep one again. Can't, though. Against building policies."

"Mrs. Gaston has a dog," I said. "She lives across the hall from Grandma's old apartment. Her dog's an apricot poodle named Beatrice."

Mr. Wilkes shook his head. "Mrs. Gaston *had* a dog. Building managers made her get rid of it."

*"What?!"* Chelsie almost exploded.

"It's true. This fall they told her, get rid of the dog or get out. Old lady like that can't pick up and move. Had to find a home for poor old Beatrice."

Chels put down her sandwich and roared: *"That's outrageous!"*

Everyone in the restaurant turned to look. My face went pink. Mr. Wilkes, however, didn't look embarassed.

"I'll say it's outrageous. But what can you do?"

All three of us picked up our sandwiches and ate silently.

Since Bullrush was actually my cat, I got to carry him to the ring when our number came up. My heart felt like it would pop.

The judge was a big man. He had started out looking crisp in a tie and a jacket, but by now he was starting to look a little sweaty. He had taken off his coat, and his tie was open at the neck and crooked.

He held up each entry as it was being judged and announced its name: Sing-Sing, a Siamese with stripes on his back legs; Mrs. Fancycats, an all-black longhair with one comma-shaped spot of white over one eye; Herb, a skin-and-bones grey with baggy skin. He reached into cage seventy-one.

"Here, at the other end of the spectrum, we have a tubby male named Bullrush."

The audience tittered.

"He's not *fat*," I hissed to Chelsie.

"I don't begrudge him a few extra pounds," the judge said into his microphone. "Believe me, folks, I know how much fun it is to get into that condition."

When the judge felt his bone structure, and passed his hand down his back, Bullrush arched up and purred so loud you could have heard it in the back row. The audience loved it.

"One gorgeous cat," said Mr. Wilkes, leaning toward me. "What's his secret?"

"Cod liver oil," I whispered back.

Bullrush sat on my lap during the rest of the judging. Then it was time for semifinals. Chelsie's fingernails dug into my arm while the steward put the numbers on the kennels. The second to the last number up was seventy-one!

"I knew it! I knew it!" cried Mr. Wilkes.

I rushed back to the judging ring with Bullrush draped over my arm. He was very relaxed. At least one of us was. I put him in his cage and went back to my seat.

Semifinals went like lightning. The friendly judge stepped to the microphone.

"Ladies and gentlemen . . . our lovely Queen of Household Pets: Bo Peep. And her royal counterpart: King El Gato! Let's give them a hand."

Chelsie looked crushed. Come to think of it, I didn't feel so hot, either. I clapped, though, like a good sport. That was that.

"Hold on, folks," the judge continued, after the applause had died down. "The royal court isn't complete without runners-up. Let me also introduce the pristine Princess Lenora, and the handsome Prince of Household Pets, the ample-bodied Bullrush!"

The room exploded with applause.

"That's us!" shouted Chelsie, nudging me out of my chair.

Bullrush got a little plastic crown with an elastic chin strap. Somebody took pictures. I don't know if it was the newspaper or not.

"I told you," Chelsie gloated. "All he needed was a good bath."

"Congratulations," said Mr. Wilkes, extending his hand solemnly. "You deserved to win. That's one impressive cat."

Mr. Wilkes drove us home. Mom and Dad made a big fuss. There was strawberry shortcake for everyone, with a cup of coffee on the side. Bullrush, the star, got a bowl of real cream and crushed strawberries. He licked around the strawberries, but he liked the cream just fine.

"At this rate," said Chels, watching him delicately clean his face afterward, "that cat'll never lose weight."

# 15

After a really great weekend, school is an even bigger letdown than usual. On Monday I was really depressed. An all-time low.

Corey smiled at me when he came into Mrs. Hartford's room—on time! It was his usual strange, crooked, and slightly scary smile. I smiled back, and I saw that some of the people in the class noticed, too. Jennifer Meyerhauser, for one, the rat.

Mrs. Hartford plunged right in. I concentrated hard, looking so diligent you wouldn't have believed it.

I shouldn't have been surprised about the note. It landed right in front of me, and everyone turned to look. *Thank you, Jennifer Meyerhauser*, I thought angrily, flashing her a look and slapping the note into my book. She just blinked innocently.

Corey and I were on our best behavior, but I was itching for class to be over. Corey, too, because as soon as the bell rang, he was gone, laughing with his wild friends.

Jennifer was standing by her chair gabbing when I came up behind her and called her name.

She turned around. "Oh, hi."

"I need to talk to you."

Her friends drifted out the door, probably to practice cheers or something.

"You sent me all those notes, didn't you? Including this one: 'Give him up. Corey Talbott is not the one for you.' You're the mad note writer."

"Well," she said, looking at the door as if it was her only escape. "Not exactly."

"I have witnesses!"

She looked uncomfortable, and glanced around. "All I can tell you is it wasn't my idea."

"Whose was it, then?"

"Look, I *told* you I can't say. What does it matter who sent them? Just forget about it."

"It's killing me," I said. "And it's stupid."

"Okay, I'll tell you, but you can't let anyone know. I didn't write those notes; it was Hilary Clifford. She found out you were in my second-period class."

"And my fourth."

90

"She wanted me to give 'em to you. She didn't know Corey was actually going to start *liking* you."

"Huh?"

"Well, she *saw* you with him in the main office."

I started to laugh.

"So, do you like him or what?"

I just kept laughing.

"Vickie, you're as strange as Hilary," said Jennifer, and waltzed out of the room, almost bumping into Peggy, who was on her way in.

"*Hi*, Vickie! I've been looking all over for you. What were you talking to Jennifer about? I didn't know you were friends."

We joined the flow of bodies in the hallway. Peggy talked a mile a minute.

"Hey, how's your brother? I think he's the *cew*-test thing! I saw you yesterday in the office! What were you doing down there? What's Corey Talbott like? I think he's the *cew*-test thing!"

I couldn't squeeze a word in. I started working with my locker combination.

"Hilary wants me to see if you're still coming on the Wisconsin weekend. She wants to know *today*; don't ask me why. Are you? It'll be fun. You, me, Hilary, and Chelsie. And my parents, of course, but we'll deal with that later. Can you come?"

"I don't know yet. My parents, you know."

"Well, find out!" She dodged across the hall, waving.

"Hi, kiddo," Chels said, attacking her combination. "How's the owner of the most royal cat in Minnesota?"

"Listen, Chels. Big news. I found out who's been writing the notes."

"No! Who?"

"Hilary Clifford."

"Hilary? What does *she* know about Corey? I know for a fact she's never even talked to him. She's afraid to. So how would she—?"

"I think she made everything up. She thought I'd fall for a phony story about Corey liking me and make a fool of myself."

"Story, nothing. You and Corey are like this." Chels held up her fingers, crossed.

"We had one conversation, Chelsie. That's it."

"That's more than Hilary's done," said Chels, fishing out her home ec notebook. "I'd say you really pulled a fast one on her."

She slammed her locker. "I'm mad, Vic. And I'm going to get to the bottom of this."

# 16

Mom and Dad raked while Matthew and I stuffed big plastic bags with the season's last leaves. It was getting dark and cold, and my hands were stiff. No one was talking much, except Matthew, who was singing the song about the lady who swallowed a fly.

After about the fortieth verse, Mom blurted out suddenly, "Your father and I are going away—just overnight. We'll leave Friday after work, and come home Saturday evening. Can you take care of things here, Victoria?"

I pushed another armload of leaves into the bag. "I guess so," I said.

"Good. I'll have the Johnstons check in on you, of

course. But if you can handle one evening alone, I guess we'll take off."

Dad didn't say anything. He kept raking with strong strokes.

"Where are you going?" Matthew asked.

"North," said Mom. "The Swansons from church are letting us use their cabin on the North Shore."

"What about work?" I said. "Dad can't just abandon the restaurant."

He looked at me, puzzled. "I've already made arrangements," he said. "They'll manage."

I didn't like the sound of this trip. Maybe they'd decide to get a divorce while they were gone. I was going to make up more excuses why they couldn't go, but Matthew interrupted.

"Can't I come along?" he asked.

"No, honey, not this time." Mom put her arm around him and squeezed. She didn't look happy.

"Okay, but make Vickie promise she won't boss me around." He crossed his arms and glared at me.

"Matthew, brother, dear, I wouldn't dream of bossing you around. Matter of fact, I'll let you watch all your favorite TV shows."

" 'Love Boat'?" he asked suspiciously.

*That* stupid show!

"Yes," I said. "Even 'Love Boat.' "

"Oh, boy!"

"And I'll make popcorn. *With* butter."

"Oh, boy!"

Dad flashed me a grateful look and a wink. Then

he concentrated on the leaves that had collected under the shrubs.

I helped Matthew make a big pile of slightly soggy leaves, trying not to eye Mom and Dad too carefully.

Things had been going so good! I had thought our troubles were over! It goes to show how wrong a person can be.

I heard the phone ringing faintly and dropped my rake. "I'll get it!" I yelled too loudly, brushing off some clinging leaves.

"Hello?" I asked breathlessly, hoping it was Chels.

"Hi," said a voice. "This is Peter. You know. Peter."

"Oh, hi." I had forgotten all about old Peter. I was glad to hear his voice.

"I just called to find out how things are." He swallowed and stopped. He was acting awfully nervous. "So . . . how are things?"

"Terrible," I said. "Terrible, terrible, terrible."

"Are your parents arguing?"

"Worse than that, Peter. They're going away together on Friday. They're going somewhere overnight. Probably a last-ditch effort to patch things up."

"My parents went away for a whole week before they got a divorce. It didn't do any good. Hey, I'm really sorry, Vickie. That's too bad."

Suddenly I felt like I was going to cry. I didn't

say anything, because I was afraid I'd let loose. Which would have been disastrous.

"Well, there's nothing I can do, I guess. But I wanted you to know that anytime you need to go canoeing or walking around or anything, you can just ask."

"Thanks, Peter," I said. "I'll let you know."

# 17

I noticed Ms. Runebach's new haircut right off the bat. She was leaning against the wall, and I was in a line, being pushed toward the cafeteria. I waved, but she was looking for someone in the other direction. Probably Mr. Dahl. If I got her attention, I'd tell her that I thought her haircut was very attractive. I bet her students hadn't even noticed. That's the trouble with teaching.

Suddenly I heard my name. It was Ms. Runebach. She was looking for *me*. She motioned with her finger.

When I finally got across the hall, she leaned down. "Come to my class after school, okay? I have something important to talk to you about."

At lunch I sat with some kids I kind of knew, and saved a place for Chels. Pretty soon she showed up, breathless.

"Guess what, Vic, old pal. I asked her!" Her cheeks were flushed, as though she'd been running. "I walked right up to Hilary Clifford and I said, "Hey, what's the deal, kid?'"

"You did not!"

"Sure, I did. Why not? You can't go around being weak kneed about this stuff. You've got to stand right up and go for the gusto."

"What did she say?"

A little enthusiasm left her face. "Well, she wouldn't tell me much. Matter of fact, she denied everything."

"That's going for the gusto, all right."

Peggy found an empty spot across the table and plopped down. "Hi, you all."

The noise level was climbing. As more kids poured in, we practically had to shout.

"Jennifer told me," said Peggy, leaning close across the table. "She said Hilary's been sending those notes to you. Really, Vickie, I didn't know she was doing that. I would never have let her."

"I don't get it," I said. "How come Hilary would go to all that trouble to send those notes? It doesn't make sense."

"She doesn't like you for some reason, I guess."

"The skiing weekend isn't going to be much fun," I said gloomily.

98

"That's another problem. She kept asking if you two were going on the skiing trip and I kept saying I didn't know and she said well she wasn't going if you were going. And I said that was sure stupid, and she didn't *have* to come. So I invited Jennifer instead!" She finished triumphantly and crossed her arms.

"Wow," said Chels.

I had to hand it to Peggy. She hadn't turned out so bad after all. Maybe Chelsie and I were having a good influence on her.

"I bet Hilary is mad," I said.

"Hopping mad. Fighting mad. Burning mad." said Chels.

"She's just jealous!" Peggy said. "Now you guys *have* to come."

*Maybe*, I thought with a silent groan, *maybe I could avoid my locker for the rest of my life. Maybe I'll never have to see Hilary again. Maybe—*

But, as usual, I had to make a trip to my locker to get my afternoon books. I had decided to ignore Hilary Clifford if I saw her.

"Hi, Vickie!" There she was, calling to me from across the hall, cheerful as can be.

"Hi."

"What did you think of my little joke?" she asked. "I really had you going, didn't I?"

I took a breath. "Actually, I don't think it was much of a joke. I also don't think it was a very nice thing to do." Miraculously, my voice didn't shake.

99

"You got me into a lot of trouble."

Hilary shurgged. "Well, I don't care if you believe it was a joke or not. It was."

I didn't feel like arguing. I just wanted to get out of there. I shut my locker and walked away, trying not to hate Hilary. It was hard.

I couldn't wait to get home after school, but I had promised Ms. Runebach I would stop by her office. I fought my way down the crowded hallway. Lockers were slamming and everyone was yelling, "See you tomorrow." The buses in the drive were orange, noisy blurs.

I headed toward the English department.

"Hi, there!" called Ms. Runebach when I opened the door to her room and went inside. "You don't look like your usual chipper self. Is everything okay?"

For a minute, I was ready to blab everything, but I was afraid she'd be sympathetic. When people get sympathetic with me, I tend to cry. I didn't want to cry in front of Ms. Runebach.

"Pretty okay," I said, and sat down on the chair next to hers.

"Pretty okay's better than dreadful, at least."

I felt the corners of my lips turn up. Good ole Ms. Runebach.

"I like your haircut," I said. "It's pretty flashy."

"Is it?" Ms. Runebach put her hand up to touch her hair, and blushed. "It's short, I know that much. Thank you, Vickie." She cleared her throat and rustled a few papers on her desk. "Actually, there's a reason for calling you in here. It's about a small matter. A matter involving Helen Hartford."

*Helen who? Hartford? Oh.* I realized who she meant. *Wouldn't you know her name would be Helen?*

"I hear the two of you had a little . . . squabble a few days ago."

"Yeah," I said. The anger started up again, suddenly. What right did Ms. Runebach have nosing into my problems? Between my parents and Hilary and my teachers I didn't have any privacy at all. I glared at Ms. Runebach's kneecaps.

"When Helen described the situation to me, I couldn't believe it. I *told* her I didn't believe it. I said you'd been in my class for an entire year and you had always, well, almost always, been a model student. A *star* pupil, matter of fact."

I found a hangnail on my left index finger and picked it.

". . . But she was insistent. So I wanted to get the full story from you." She sat back, waiting.

I was sick of telling the story. But for the hundredth time I gave the details, from the beginning.

Ms. Runebach was smiling. "I *knew* I was right about you, Vickie. There's only one thing to do. Talk to Mrs. Hartford."

I gasped, almost swallowing my gum.

"Maybe you could talk to her," I said.

"I think that's your responsibility, Vickie. Mostly I'm concerned that the mishap doesn't go on your record, especially because of the Scholastic Essay Contest. Besides, I can't talk to Helen. It would look like we've been whispering behind her back. I happen to know that Helen has been going through a rough time, Vickie. I don't want to add any more stress to her life."

"I've been going through a rough time, too, Ms. Runebach, but I'm not mean! Just because life is hard doesn't mean that she can treat people mean!"

"I know, Vickie, I know. I'm sorry." She hesitated, delicately. "*Are* you going through a hard time? I'm sorry to hear that. You're okay, aren't you?"

The tears brimmed at the edges of my eyes. "Excuse me, Ms. Runebach, I've got to go now." I pushed back the chair and made a dash for the door.

That sympathy gets me every time.

# 18

"Uh-oh," said Chels when she saw me. "Catastrophe." No one reads a face like Chelsie.

She had my locker open, and I grimaced at her and tossed my books inside. "Not catastrophe, exactly. Just doom and despair."

"Don't ask, right?"

"Right."

We took the long-cut home, through the shopping center parking lot, across the ravine, and up through the woods.

The air smelled good—like clean, cold lake air. I felt a little better. Chels started telling me about this new brilliant idea of hers.

"It's a letter of complaint, Vic. I'm sending it to

Mr. Wilkes's landlord, protesting the no-pets rule. I think people at The Towers should get to have pets if they want them. This is what I have so far:

*Dear Landlord:*

*Dogs are great with burglars. Cats catch mice and insects. Pets make people very, very happy. So why don't you allow pets at The Towers? We're writing this letter to urge you—*

What do you think of that, Vic, *urge?*

*—urge you to reconsider. Let pets into The Towers!*

*Please take a look at the petition enclosed. It is signed by people who live in the building. As you can see, only a FEW—*

Underlined *and* capitalized, Vic.

*—only a FEW people think the no pets rule is a good one. Most of them think it really stinks. (No pun intended.) A couple of them even told us they don't plan to stick around if they don't see action fast!*

*As you can see by our petition, most people*

*would be willing to pay a few extra dollars a*
*month so that they could keep a dog or cat.*
*Think about that!*

*We are referring especially to Mrs. Gaston's*
*dog, Beatrice. Bring Beatrice back!*

*Respectfully,*

*Chelsie Bixler,*
*president*
*Bring Back Animals Real Kwik! (BARK)*

*Victoria "Vic" Mahoney*
*co-president*

"That was the best I could do for the "k" in
BARK. Aside from that, what do you think?" Chels
grinned, showed all the metal in her teeth.

"My dad says you can't fight city hall," I said.

"You're being a gloom ball, again, Vic. How can
we lose? With all those signatures, the manage-
ment at The Towers will have to say yes. You can't
beat majority rule. That's what I always say."

"Well, it is a good idea," I said. "But if we do it at
The Towers, we have to do it over at Willowood,
too. Mom herself said pets would be good therapy
for the people who live there. And my friend Mr.
Smith could use a pet."

"Right-o!" said Chels, making a note in her

folder. "Let's go over to your house and plan this thing out."

When Matthew found out what we were doing, he wanted to help. I rolled my eyes and tried with all my might to think of a reason why he couldn't help.

"Okay, you can help," I told him. "But you have to let the president and co-president do the talking."

"I'll be secretary-treasurer," he volunteered, jumping up and down.

Imagine someone *wanting* to be the secretary-treasurer. We took him up on it, even though he couldn't write much more than his name.

Chels chewed on her pen. "What day should we get signatures on the petition?"

"Wait a minute. I thought you already did that."

Chelsie's face was a blank. "What made you think that?"

"You said in your letter that almost all the residents of The Towers wouldn't mind a hike in their rent if they could keep pets!"

"Oh, I wrote the letter first. Now we need to collect the data."

The president of BARK is way too optimistic. Luckily, the co-president is a little more realistic.

We set the petition day for Saturday—the Saturday my parents were gone. We agreed to meet at our house, nine o'clock sharp.

# 19

"You'll lock all the windows and doors?" Dad grilled me Friday night. "Make sure the stove is off? Not let any strangers in?"

"Oh, sure, Dad. Like I'm suddenly going to start letting strangers in the house."

He shook my shoulder gently. "Just testing you. You'll be fine."

Mom appeared, looking comfortable in her old jeans and one of Dad's flannel shirts. "Now be sure to lock all the windows and doors, okay? And don't forget to turn the oven off after you use it—"

Dad and I looked at each other.

"—and Bixlers' number is on the note pad in the kitchen by the phone."

"Mom! Chelsie Bixler is my best friend. Don't you think I memorized her number about twenty years ago?"

"Oh! Oh, right. I suppose so. Remember, Mrs. Johnston is going to check in on you. Well, then, are we all set?"

Matthew showed up just in time to say good-bye. He didn't look upset. He looked kind of happy, as a matter of fact. I glared at him suspiciously. There was definitely mischief in his eyes. He thought he was going to get away with murder while Mom and Dad were away.

" 'Bye, Mom. 'Bye, Dad. Bring me a souvenir, okay?"

"We'll only be gone until tomorrow night," Dad protested, opening the squeaky door to the garage. "You'd think our children were glad to get rid of us!"

Mom blew more kisses, and they got into the car and drove off.

I made us a frozen pizza for dinner, the one I had goaded Mom into buying for us. It's the kind of food we don't get to eat while my parents are around because Mom is into healthy stuff and Dad says it's a sacrilege to eat imitation food.

Matthew and I loved it. Stringy cheese everywhere. And Pepsi. And all in front of the TV.

The phone rang.

"Hello, Victoria. This is your very, very best friend, Chelsie Bixler."

"Matthew and I just had the best dinner of our lives." Talking about dinner made me think of the stove. I stretched the cord over to make sure I had turned off the oven.

There was the sound of pages rustling. "I called to make last-minute plans for the petition. I'm checking off things on my organizational chart. A good committee president should always have an organizational chart. Okay now. Are you bringing pens?"

"Check."

"Extra paper?"

"Check."

"Bullrush?"

"Huh?"

"I thought maybe we should take him. You know. Make the people over at The Towers feel sentimental. No one can resist a baby or a cat."

"*I'm* not going to carry him."

"He is pretty heavy. Well, scratch Bullrush. We'll have to count on your personality to win folks over."

I could hardly hear all this because Matthew was making so much noise in the family room. It sounded as though he was moving furniture around.

"Hold on a sec," I said, and yelled at him to stop whatever it was he was doing.

"Vic," said Chels, "that was perfect. You'll make a wonderful parent someday. Listen, one more thing. I've been whittling on my mom all night. A few minutes ago I got her to admit that I'm very responsible."

"Wow. I'm sincerely impressed."

"This hasn't been easy. It's been miserable, to tell the truth. But it'll be worth it, for a kitten. I've decided to get one from the Humane Society. Don't you think that's a good idea? Those cats really need homes."

"I'll help you pick her—or him—out."

"Boy, I can't wait. This has been the hardest battle of all with my parents. The makeup issue was a hundred times easier."

I wrapped the phone cord around my bare toes, trying to think if there was any great news I was forgetting to tell her about. She beat me to it.

"Vic, did I tell you that Grant Hirshfield *talked* to me today? We had an honest-to-goodness conversation! He told me he was trying out for the football squad next year. And he asked if I liked football."

"What did you say? Did you tell him you were *mad* about sports? That you spend every waking moment going to games?"

"Actually, I told him the truth. I said I wasn't into sports that much."

I giggled. "What did *he* say?"

"He said, well maybe I could come and watch him play anyway, sometime."

"Great," I said, practically falling over laughing. "A date a year in advance! That's planning ahead!"

"Of course, then he wanted me to go get a Coke with him over at Dahlia's."

That caught my attention. Finally I got my breath back. "Did you go?" I whispered.

"Of course, I went. What am I, dumb?"

"You went to Dahlia's with Grant Hirshfield!"

"He sure is cute," said Chelsie.

I hadn't told her about Peter's last phone call yet, so I told her, leaving out the part about *why* he had called. Not that Peter was Grant Hirshfield or anything. Not that a phone call was as exciting as going to Dahlia's for a Coke. But it was the best I could do.

"This is great," said Chels, happily. "Next year we'll be double-dating to all the football games at Keats."

Boy, oh, boy. I knew my parents weren't ready for dating yet. But I'd cross that bridge later.

"You still coming over at nine tomorrow?" I asked, to change the subject.

"Sure thing. With pen and petition in hand."

"See you bright and early," I said.

"Over and out."

111

# 20

The knock at the front door came at exactly nine.

"I've got it! I've got it!" shrieked my noisy brother.

A second later, Chelsie's voice floated in from the hall.

Chels is not known for being punctual. I wasn't ready. I had to hurry up wiping the last dribbles of milk and soggy Cheerios in the kitchen.

Matthew danced back, leading Chels by the hand. One look, and I knew the president of BARK was ready to bawl.

"Don't forget, I'm the secretary-treasurer," Matthew was babbling. He looked at us suspiciously. "Remember, I get to go along."

"Right, Matthew," I said, "and as official BARK secretary-treasurer, you're in charge of supplies. We need a clipboard, paper, and some pens. Extra ones so we don't run out. Go see if you can scrounge them up."

He disappeared.

Chelsie's face crumpled immediately. "They said no. I asked Mom and Dad about the kitten, and they said absolutely not."

"Oh, no," I moaned.

"I don't even want to go through with the petition, hardly."

"How could they say no? You've been so responsible."

"Mom said animals tie you down if you want to go on vacation or anything. She said she's allergic to cat boxes. They give her the vapors. Whatever that is."

All of a sudden I was very grateful for my parents. They're weird, but at least they'd let me have a cat if my life depended on it.

"You've always got Bullrush," I offered meekly. But I knew that even a magnificent cat like Bullrush didn't make up for a cat all your own.

"I know," she said sniffing. "But I wanted to feed my cat and make it toys and name it."

"Maybe you can still talk them into it."

"No way," she said, sighing.

There was nothing else to say. Matthew appeared with handfuls of pens and a pad of notepaper from Dad's restaurant tucked under his arm.

"Guess we should head out, huh?" I asked.

"Sure, I guess so," said Chels.

Like a miniature army, Chels, Matthew, and I marched outside, ready to change the world. Or The Towers, at least.

There were a lot of apartments. By the time we got to the tenth floor, Matthew was whining, and Chelsie looked like she wanted to quit, too. I wouldn't let them. I reminded them about Mrs. Gaston and Beatrice.

"Let's stop at Mr. Wilkes's," Chels said. "We've got to take a break. My feet ache."

Mr. Wilkes's apartment was on the twenty-fifth floor. We knocked, and he came right to the door.

"What's going on?" he wanted to know.

We told him.

Mr. Wilkes thought it was a fabulous idea. "Bet you're tired out. You each deserve a lemonade. Come on in."

It didn't take much to convince us.

"How many signatures?" He held the petition away from his face. "Thirty-five? Not bad. I'll make it thirty-six. There."

He signed a flourishy signature.

"After this," I said, trying to make up for Chelsie's silence, "we're going over to Willowood. I bet *everyone* over there will sign a petition to let animals in."

114

Chelsie wasn't herself. She hardly said anything which is definitely not typical. It didn't take Mr. Wilkes long to pick that up. He made bewildered faces at me when she wasn't looking, and finally I couldn't stand it anymore.

"Chelsie's parents said 'no cat,'" I blurted. "Absolutely, positively no cat, ever."

"Reason?"

"Cats are dirty," said Chels. "They shed. They scratch on furniture. They might interfere with a trip or something."

"That's just silly," I said, getting angry again.

"Yeah!" chimed in Matthew. "Bullrush is very clean. Most of the time."

"Well, Chelsie," said Mr. Wilkes, thoughtfully, "Your parents are right, in a way. No doubt about it. It's just that people like you and me are willing to put up with a little cat hair for the privilege of caring for an animal. Hmm. Have to dwell on this dilemma."

Then he smiled, and flashed me a wink. I didn't know what that meant, but I winked back.

# 21

When Mom and Dad got home, I was watching TV and trying to do my homework at the same time. I decided to be cool. I wouldn't even *ask* them how it went. I'd just wait for the news.

Dad rushed into the family room. He grabbed me and swung me up in the air like I was two. "How's the girl?"

"Come on, Dad," I said. "Give me a break."

"See?" said Mom, dumping a suitcase on the floor. "I *told* him you'd do all right. I don't see any evidence of calamity."

"*Rat*," Dad snarled, glowering at her.

I gave them the once-over. They looked normal. They acted normal. I figured those were bad signs.

I gave them the lowdown on everything we had done while they were gone, stuff like when Matthew had gone to bed, etc. I didn't go into detail about how much we'd loved the pizza. No use stirring up trouble.

They took showers and unpacked forever. While I waited, I wished I could call someone—especially Peter. But one of them might come downstairs and hear something and that would be terrible. I sat in my chair and gritted my teeth, preparing for the worst.

But when they came back, they were smiling. They made themselves some orange cinnamon tea and sat down to watch the last part of a very dumb movie with me. Mom stroked Bullrush absent-mindedly, and Dad just sprawled lazily on the couch. The suspense was killing me. It looked like I was going to *have* to ask. During a commercial, I finally got up the guts.

"Well?"

"Well, what?" asked Dad, still concentrating on TV.

"What happened on the trip?"

"Oh, nothing much. At least, nothing disastrous. It wasn't anything like our family camping trips." Dad stretched, flashing a wicked one at Mom. "Of course, your mother did have quite a time starting the cookstove. It was very entertaining. But she managed, in the end."

"No thanks to you," said Mom. "Vickie, you

would have loved it. The place is right next to a stream. There were deer, rabbits, chipmunks, squirrels, all kinds of wildlife. It's a wonderful place. We're going to ask the Swansons if we can go back, take you kids." She paused. "But in the summer. When it warms up."

"It was perfect as is," Dad protested. "We could go next weekend, if we wanted!"

"It was cold," said Mom, taking a careful sip of tea. "I've never been so cold in all my life."

The movie was dumb. I couldn't just sit there when I didn't have any idea if my parents were going to stay married or not!

"I'm going to bed," I announced abruptly.

" 'Night, honey," Mom murmured.

"See you, baby," Dad said.

I climbed upstairs to my room.

After I had read my Bible and put on my pajamas, I sat at my desk and started to write:

*Dear Mom and Dad.*
*I can't ask you this in person. It's too embarrassing. So I'm writing you a note. I've been wondering. Are you by any chance going to get a divorce?*

I tore the note in half. It was stupid.

The night was very dark. From my bed I watched the moon's bright, washed face through the curtains for a long time. Finally I heard Dad's heavy footsteps on the stairs. He paused in the doorway.

"Baby, what's wrong? Why are you crying?"

His weight sank the mattress low on one side. He rocked me against his face.

I couldn't stop. Like I said, sympathy makes me cry. If he had stopped rocking me, I would have dried up the tears like that.

Finally he did. "Now, tell me the trouble."

I sniffed and wiped my eyes with the sheet.

"I figured everything out. I know the truth."

"Truth?"

"I know you and Mom are getting a divorce."

Dad snapped on the lamp on my desk. I squinted at his surprised face.

"That's preposterous!"

"You're not getting a divorce?"

"Absolutely not."

"But you've been fighting    ."

"Oh, Vickie—Okay, things haven't been all that great lately. That doesn't mean we've been plotting a divorce." He scratched his head. "In fact, Mom and I have more or less been sorting things out. That's why we took our little trip. To get a fresh perspective. Take time to pray and to be together."

"Oh," I said, suddenly feeling pretty foolish.

"Hold on a minute." Dad climbed back down the stairs.

I could hear him talking to Mom. Then I heard her say, "What?" and then their footsteps clattered back up the stairs.

119

"Vickie," Mom said, "this takes the cake! A divorce? We haven't been fighting that much, have we? Here I thought we were doing so well."

My mind stopped spinning. I looked at them in relief. It was starting to soak in. No divorce.

"I think we'd better spill the beans," said Dad. "Eh, Bob?"

"Spill what beans?" I asked.

Mom and Dad looked at each other.

"You tell her, Terry."

Dad put his hand on my shoulder as if he were knighting me.

"Victoria Hope Mahoney, you're about to become a big sister—again."

I should have seen it coming a hundred miles off. Talk about stupid! Stupid, stupid, stupid!

"Really?" I squeaked.

Dad grinned at my dumb look. "Believe it. It's true. In about seven months, as a matter of fact."

I wasn't upset. It was weird. Last year I would have hit the roof if I'd known we were having another baby. But it didn't bother me. It really didn't. Maybe it'd even be fun.

"Of course, a new baby complicates life, you realize," said Mom, sitting down on the edge of my bed. "It puts an even bigger financial strain on the family. I guess that's what Dad and I have been worried about. Maybe it looked as though we were mad at each other, but we were just coming to grips with a new problem."

120

"But there's no problem the Mahoneys can't face—together!" bellowed Dad, holding his arms out grandly.

The light in my room seemed bright. Everything seemed bright and new. Even Mom's eyes sparkled. It hurt my eyes.

"You look a little dazed," said Mom, smiling.

"I'll get over it," I promised. "Don't worry."

# 22

The president of *Bring Back Animals Real Kwik!* got a letter from the owners of The Towers apartment building, and I got a carbon copy. The letter said that they appreciated our efforts. It also said they had amended some rules so that residents could keep pets, providing they weighed under five pounds. It wasn't the world, but it was something. Chels pointed out that Bullrush could never make it at The Towers. He weighed ten pounds *at least*.

"We're a success, Vic," she said, thumping my back. "Now Mrs. Gaston can bring Beatrice home. With our brains, personality, and powers of persuasion, who knows how far we may go?"

"Maybe you *can* fight city hall—at least a little."

Willowood said no, flat. Well, actually what they said is they "weren't equipped to handle pets, while continuing to provide quality nursing care." That's what the letter said. But thank you for bringing this matter to their attention, Blah, blah, blah.

"You can't win 'em all," Mr. Wilkes observed when I called him with the news. "They probably have good reasons for their decision."

Why did he always have to see the other side of things?

"We can still take pets in, though, right? I could take Bullrush over there more. Everyone thinks he's the greatest."

"You could and you should," said Mr. Wilkes. "If Chelsie had a pet, *she'd* sure take it in."

That was a weird thing to say, but Mr. Wilkes has been known to say strange things.

I wasn't sure, but I thought I heard him chuckling quietly before we said good-bye and hung up.

# 23

"Er . . . Mrs. Hartford? Could I talk to you a second? It's important."

It would *have* to be important to disturb Mrs. Hartford at 7:45 on a Monday morning. That's what her face said when she looked up from the confused pile of papers she was grading. I began to get a feeling, a strong feeling. It was a feeling that said: "What are you doing here, you idiot? Run! Quick!"

"Come in," said Mrs. Hartford. Helen Hartford.

Trapped, I slumped over to her desk. I didn't sit down. That way I could leave right after I'd said what I came to say.

"Sit down," she said, pointing with her red pen. I sat down.

"I wanted to explain about the other day—"

Mrs. Hartford fingered her cameo earring. She didn't look interested in hearing my explanation for anything.

"—when you sent me down to Ms. Elk's office."

Mrs. Hartford took off her glasses and rubbed her eyes as if she were very, very tired. She had *veins* all over the bridge of her nose, tiny red veins, right next to the damp ovals where the nosepieces had been. I stared at them, almost forgetting the next part of my speech.

"I—I wanted to apologize about laughing in class. Normally I wouldn't have. Really, I wouldn't. But I was in kind of a bad mood. Because of the note."

Mrs. Hartford's eyebrows came together. "Note? Refresh my memory, please. I've had too many things on my mind lately. What note?"

Now I was supposed to tell the same old story to Mrs. Hartford? This was even worse than I had figured.

"Remember when a note got passed to me, and you read it aloud to the class?"

"Ohhh. Yes. Yes, I remember the note." She pushed back her chair and folded her big arms, and her expression changed to suspicion.

"Well, I wanted to explain. Number one, I didn't have anything to do with that note. I didn't know someone was going to pass it to me. Number two, I was angry because you had embarrassed me. That's why I was laughing that day in class. I shouldn't have been. I'm sorry. That's what I came to say."

I hoped Ms. Runebach was happy now.

"I appreciate the apology. Nevertheless, I don't allow note passing in class."

"I *never* pass notes," I said.

"We'll wipe the slate clean. Just don't let it happen again."

I guess my mouth was hanging open. She wasn't even listening! How could I keep it from happening again, if I wasn't the one passing the notes? It didn't make sense.

I stood up. "All right," I said.

"Thanks for coming in, Victoria," said Mrs. Hartford, not looking up from the paper she had picked up.

"You're welcome, Mrs. Hartford," I said.

I had done the right thing, I knew that. But it didn't feel all that great.

# 24

Maybe Chelsie's parents felt guilty about the cat or something. All I know is they didn't blink twice about the Wisconsin weekend.

Chels waited for me after gym class to report. "Of course, they wanted to make sure it was chaperoned and all. But when I told them Mr. and Mrs. Hiltshire were going to be there, they said, okay. I said it'd be good exercise and *full* of fresh air. Parents like that kind of stuff.

"I'm going to get a great big sweater with reindeer on it. If you're going to sit around the lodge drinking hot spiced cider you've got to have a big sweater. Leg warmers wouldn't hurt, either."

She turned a sudden, stern look on me. "You've

*got* to ask your parents. You can't stall any longer. Peg needs to know."

"I'll ask tonight. Mom and Dad are in very good moods all of a sudden."

"No wonder. A baby!"

Corey Talbott ran by with his wild friends, Paul Wong and Russell Randolph. He kind of hung back when he saw me.

"Hi," he said, sort of waving. "See you in science."

Chelsie let out her breath. She must have been holding it. "Wow! You really *are* friends with him. No wonder Hilary is mad! You're friends with the coolest guy in school."

"Ho hum," I said, shining my fingernails on my shirt sleeve.

That night I got home earlier than usual. *Responsibly* early. Mom had taken the day off, so she was home. But she didn't look up from the cookbook she was studying.

"How come you're reading a cookbook?" I asked, forgetting for a minute how nervous I was. "You hate cooking."

"I don't hate cooking. I'm just smart enough to admit I'm not culinarily gifted. If you have to know, I'm looking for Thanksgiving recipes."

"Mom, Thanksgiving is *weeks* away."

"I figure if I start practicing now, by then I'll have some dishes down well enough to impress your father."

Gross. I hate it when my parents are romantic.

"How does this sound? Cranberry-Walnut Relish?"

"*Mom!*"

"Okay. Here's another. Yams in honey raisin sauce. Or this. Broiled tomato-eggplant casserole."

"Yuck!"

"I made that last one up."

My mother definitely has a sadistic streak.

"Tell you what, Mom. I'll set the table while you look for better recipes. Edible recipes." I made a dive for the silverware.

Mom whistled. "Hoo, boy. Someone's acting mighty peculiar."

I had the table set and had even done some dusting when Dad walked in, rubbing his cold hands.

"What are you doing here?" Mom and I asked together. He was supposed to be making steaks for the dinner rush.

He grinned mysteriously. "A little fancy talking, some time swapping . . . Aren't you glad to see me?"

"Thrilled." Mom sounded as though she meant it.

He pulled an envelope from his pocket, and handed it to Mom. "How far do you suppose we can make a paycheck stretch?" he asked cheerfully.

"You'd be surprised," said Mom with a smile.

Boy. I didn't know if I could take all this happy

stuff. It's a pain when your parents are too optimistic. But it was nice to have Dad home for dinner.

Usually dinner is the best time to bring up stuff like Wisconsin skiing parties. Even Matthew knows it. One time at dinner he wanted to know if he could go over to Barbie Polinski's house. He wanted to swing on her tire swing. He might have had them if he hadn't let it slip that the swing went over the lake, and that he planned to jump off. My parents said no! Absolutely not! But then they invited Barbie over to make chocolate chip cookies.

I was busily making plans to slyly bring up skiing, but the timing had to be perfect.

"I'm training in another assistant at the restaurant," Dad was saying, passing me a plate of sourdough bread. "He was a fine bus boy and a great waiter, but he's impossible in the kitchen. Sometimes I wish people would stick to their levels of expertise."

Mom shot me a miserable look. There went her cranberry-walnut relish.

"Oh, I don't know, Dad," I said, carefully. "Don't you think it's good when people stretch themselves a little? You know, try new things?"

Mom nodded vigorously.

"I mean, how do you know you can do something until you've given it a shot?"

"Well—" said Dad, grouchily.

Mom thumped her fist on the table. "Hear, hear. I agree with Vickie."

130

"I don't," said Matthew. "I tried to ride Lisa Eriksen's two-wheeler today, and I was no good. I kept falling over."

I hurried on. "So I think it'd be a good experience for me to go on a skiing weekend I was invited to."

"Skiing weekend?" repeated Dad, absent-mindedly buttering his bread. He hadn't caught on.

"Peggy Hiltshire invited me. Her parents said she could ask some friends on this skiing vacation over Christmas. They're driving a van to Wisconsin."

"*Downhill* skiing?" Mom put down her fork. "How can you even suggest such a thing?"

"Oh, Mom. Skiing is very safe. And it's *good* for you."

"Not if you break a leg. Or *both* legs."

"I'm not going to break a leg."

"If I remember right, that's what you said last year before the church ice-skating outing."

"That was a sprain. A very small sprain."

"Same difference," said Mom, picking up her fork again. "No skiing! Absolutely not! No way!"

"Who's going on this skiing weekend?" Dad asked.

"Peggy's parents, for a start. Peggy's sister. Then Peggy, Jennifer Meyerhauser, and Chelsie. And me, if you say okay. It's the last weekend before school starts again. I'd be very careful. I'll wear *two* pairs of long underwear if you want. Just say yes."

"No," said Mom. She wasn't being funny.

"Honey, we don't have the money to send you on a skiing weekend."

"That's the great thing about this, Dad. No money! The Hiltshires have a condominium there, so it's free."

"What about meals?"

"Well—"

"And ski rental?"

"I'll save up." But I didn't even have to look at Dad to know that the weekend was off. I'd never be able to save enough, even if I baby-sat every night of the week.

"I'm sorry," Dad said.

He really did sound sorry, but it didn't help.

"I never get to do anything!" I said, dangerously close to crying.

Suddenly Dad looked as though he might cry, too. "If there were anything I could do—" he said. Then he started to smile. "I'm getting an idea, a real Mahoney inspiration. All we need is a little time to plan. Why can't we have our own skiing trip—cross-country—next Christmas vacation?"

"Dad," I said, "that's a whole year away!"

"Just listen. I'll take some time off, Mom will take some time off, and we'll invite a group of your friends. We'll bribe the Swansons into letting us use the cabin for a few days. Sleeping bags, singing around the fireplace . . . How does that sound?"

"Brrr," said Mom, warming her hands over the

meat loaf. "Sounds cold to me."

"What do you think, Vickie, old girl? You can plan the whole thing."

It was a sort of good idea.

"I could decide the meals ahead? Chili, waffles?"

"Anything you want . . . within reason, of course. I'll supervise the menu preparation all myself. Gourmet ski-trip fare."

"Okay, for gourmet food, I'll go," said Mom, holding up her hand like a volunteer. "And Matthew can be in charge of after-hours entertainment. You'll have to take your harmonica, Matthew."

It was too much—the idea of sitting around a fireplace with all my friends from school while Matthew belted out "Swanee River" on the harmonica. I broke up. Mom and Dad smiled, too. It didn't make not going *this* year any better, but at least it was something to look forward to.

Maybe Chelsie would offer to skip Peggy's skiing trip, too. Then maybe I could bear the disappointment. I imagined her announcing her decision to an assembled, open-mouthed group: Jennifer, Hilary, Peggy . . . "If Vic doesn't go, I don't go. It wouldn't be any fun without my buddy, Vic."

My old buddy Chelsie made a surprise appearance after dinner.

"Hi!" she said when Dad called me to the door. "I— What's wrong?"

"I'm going out!" I shouted, grabbing my coat off the hook.

"—home by eight thirty!" Dad yelled back before I slammed the door shut.

"You look terrible!"

"Thank you very much," I said, oozing sarcasm.

"You know what I mean."

"The skiing weekend is off. They said no."

"Vic, you're kidding!"

"I wouldn't kid about this."

"But I can't believe it. It won't be half as fun without you."

Boy, was I stupid to have thought Chelsie wouldn't go without me. It was depressing to think that she'd get to go to Wisconsin and I wouldn't—it was more depressing than a conversation with Mrs. Hartford, which is pretty bad.

"Come on, Vic. I know something that'll cheer you up. I'm heading over to see Mr. Wilkes. Want to come? He said he needs help making gingersnaps."

It was an extremely cold November evening, time to stop messing around and get out mittens and scarves. Minnesota is like that. One day you're toasty and fine. The next day, bam! It's freezing.

We took the elevator up and knocked at Mr. Wilkes's door. The door creaked open. It was creepy, like a haunted house movie. Then—out came a kitten!

It was white and grey, with long hair and a crooked tail. It sniffed our feet.

134

Needless to say, Chels almost went wild.

"Get in here," said Mr. Wilkes, motioning to us, "before you have all the neighbors calling the police."

"What's her name?" Chels asked, curling her arms around the kitten.

"No name. You name her. She's mostly yours, anyway. I'm letting you adopt her, Chelsie. Of course, she'll have to sleep here. But you'll be her real owner."

It was a great idea. I really had to hand it to Mr. Wilkes. I would have hugged him, but I hadn't known him long enough yet. You have to work up to hugging, gradually. Chelsie did hug him.

"She'll shed like crazy, of course. But the clerk at the Humane Society assured me that she'd stop growing at exactly five pounds. What do you think of her?"

"Beautiful! Perfect!"

The kitten loved Chels best right off the bat. She liked me all right, but Chelsie was the cat's pajamas as far as that kitten was concerned, which was okay with me. Bullrush is kind of the jealous type.

While the gingersnaps were baking, Chels had a "fit of inspiration." That's what she called it.

"I dub thee Penzance," she said regally, "for my favorite Gilbert and Sullivan play."

It was a strange name, if you ask me. But I was so glad she had a cat, I didn't care.

The cookies came out of the oven, sparkling with

sugar. They made the whole apartment smell like ginger and Christmastime. We each ate three.

Then Mr. Wilkes pushed back his chair and announced, "It's late—grab your coats. Wilkes's Instant Chauffeur Service leaving in five minutes."

While he drove, Mr. Wilkes joked around. He said he'd will Penzance to Chelsie when he died. Her parents couldn't refuse a cat if it was willed to her, he said.

I wondered if he had any bright ideas about weekend skiing trips.

# 25

"Mom! Dad!" I yelled, pounding up the stairs to Matthew's room. "Can I please, please, please be excused from painting?"

Mom sat back on her haunches, clutching her brush. She rubbed an ear itch with her sleeve. "We're almost done here, I guess. What's up?"

"I can't explain right now. Peter's on the phone. He's *waiting*."

"Well, scrub your face before you go anywhere. There's Pacific Lagoon latex on your forehead."

I ran back downstairs.

"Sure, Peter," I said. "I'm not busy. What do you want to do? It's snowing, so canoeing is out." It was supposed to be a joke.

"Meet me in your front yard in fifteen minutes," he said. "And wear warm clothes!"

I not only wore warm clothes (long underwear), I wore eye shadow!

I saw Peter coming a long way off. His arms were loaded with stuff.

"Skis!" I shouted.

"Not just skis. Cross-country skis."

They looked like everyday kind of skis to me.

"Here," he said, passing a pair to me. "You can use mine; I'll use my dad's. They're a little long, but not too. Dad's kind of short."

He showed me how to strap everything on, and how to hold the poles. Then he showed me how to push-glide. We cross-country skiied right where the sidewalk used to be.

"Not bad!" he yelled as I push-glided down the street. "You're a natural."

Even Mom wouldn't object to *cross-country* skiing. It was much safer than downhill. And good exercise. Not to mention full of fresh air.

Peter was a pretty fancy skiier. He showed me where some trails were by his house, by the woods. We weren't a bit cold. Skiing'll make you work up a sweat every time.

We ended up back in front of my house, and I invited Peter in for a snack. I am not exactly a star in home ec, but I figured I could handle a little cocoa.

I was in such a good mood, I even made enough

138

for Matthew. The three of us sat around in the family room laughing at a pretty silly TV show. When Mom and Dad came downstairs, I whipped up more cocoa.

Peter, I noticed, kept checking Mom and Dad out. I had forgotten to tell him that the divorce had been a false alarm. As a matter of fact, they'd been pretty lovey-dovey all of a sudden. It was enough to make you sick.

"Since you're in such a good mood," said Mom in the voice she only uses when she's trying to con me into drying the dishes or vacuum, "maybe you could do a favor for your mother. If *I* were already wet from being out in the snow, *I'd* go get the mail. But since I'm not—"

"Okay, okay," I said. It was risky leaving Peter alone with Mom and Dad. They might ask him if he was my *boyfriend* or something. But I went to the front hall and pulled on my boots.

I had to stand in a drift to reach the mailbox. Back in the house, I slammed the door behind me and checked out the envelopes. Sweepstakes. Bills. A postcard from the vet saying Bullrush was due for his shots. And an envelope addressed to "Honeybunch Mahoney."

*Hilary! That rat!* Now she was going to start bugging me at home. I was mad. Really mad. If she thought I was going to fall for that stuff again—

I ripped open the envelope and quickly unfolded the note.

My darling wife, Bobbie—
Sweetheart! The news is wonderful, after all.
And so are you! God saw us through
another one, didn't he? I love
you! I love you!! I love you!!!

Terry

I blinked.

*What a relief,* I thought, folding the paper back
up, *a love letter that isn't for me.*

I went back to the family room. Maybe Peter felt
like another whip around the block.

# JUST VICTORIA

# I am absolutely *dreading* junior high.

Vic and her best friend, Chelsie, have heard enough gory details about seventh grade to ruin their entire summer vacation. And as if school weren't a big enough worry, Vic suddenly finds problems at every turn:

- Chelsie starts hanging around Peggy Hiltshire, queen of all the right cliques, who thinks life revolves around the cheerleading squad.
- Vic's mom gets a "fulfilling" new job—with significantly less pay—at a nursing home.
- Grandma Warden is looking tired and pale—and won't see a doctor.

But Victoria Hope Mahoney has a habit of underestimating her own potential. The summer brings a lot of change, but Vic is equal to it as she learns more about her faith, friendship, and growing up.

### Don't miss any books in
### The Victoria Mahoney Series!

SHELLY NIELSEN lives in Minneapolis, Minnesota, with her husband and two Yorkshire terriers.

# TAKE A BOW, VICTORIA

# I might as well die of embarrassment right here.

Victoria is finding plenty to cringe about these days, such as her hugely pregnant mom waddling into the school auditorium in full view of all Vic's friends. (Couldn't she sit quietly at home till the baby arrives?) Or such as Isadora, her flashy grand-mother, actually volunteering as set designer for the spring production at school. (Couldn't she bake cookies and knit like a normal grandma?)

Meanwhile Vic is struggling with her own con-fusing wish to be a star . . . and to stay safely hidden backstage. As some important events change life for the Mahoney family, Vic finds her ideas of stardom—and of courage—changing, too.

### Don't miss any books in
### The Victoria Mahoney Series!

#1 Just Victoria     #4 Only Kidding, Victoria
#2 More Victoria     #5 Maybe It's Love, Victoria
#3 Take a Bow, Victoria     #6 Autograph, Please, Victoria

SHELLY NIELSEN lives in Minneapolis, Minnesota, with her husband and two Yorkshire terriers.

# ONLY KIDDING, VICTORIA

## You've got to be kidding!

Spend the summer at a resort lodge in Minnesota . . . with her *family?* When she's been looking forward to endless days of good times with her new friends from school?

Victoria can't believe her parents are serious, but nothing she can do or say will change their minds. It's off to Little Raccoon Lake, a nowhere place where she's sure there will be nothing to do.

But the summer holds a lot of surprises—like Nina, one year older and a whole lot tougher, who scoffs at rules . . . and at Vic for bothering to keep them. And the bittersweet pang that comes with each letter from her best friend, Chelsie, reminding Vic of what she's missing back home. But the biggest surprise is Victoria's discovery of some things that have been right under her nose all along. . . .

### Don't miss any books in
### The Victoria Mahoney Series!

#1 Just Victoria          #4 Only Kidding, Victoria
#2 More Victoria          #5 Maybe It's Love, Victoria
#3 Take a Bow, Victoria   #6 Autograph, Please,
                             Victoria

SHELLY NIELSEN lives in Minneapolis, Minnesota, with her husband and two Yorkshire terriers.